PRAISE FOR

Achieving on Purpose:
Your GUIDE to Managerial Success

—————————————— ⋏ ——————————————

"*Achieving on Purpose* is a rich compilation of management gold! Simonds outlines a clean roadmap to success with the perfect balance of actionable strategies and supporting detail. It's a valuable and handy reference for today's manager."

-Lee J. Colan, Ph.D. Author
Stick With It: Mastering the Art of Adherence and
Engaging the Hearts and Minds of all your Employees
www.theLgroup.com

"There's an old proverb that states, 'What has been will be again, what has been done will be done again; there is nothing new under the sun.' While that statement may be generally true, Donald E. Simonds' book, *Achieving on Purpose:* Your GUIDE to Managerial Success, is definitely an exception. Most text books on management present topics over a series of books and courses, making it difficult for students to integrate and implement concepts. In contrast Simonds offers a useful way to synthesize concepts and application in a manner that allows students to grasp and use all aspects of management in one tightly organized and easy to read text. He does this by organizing topics around several very imaginative acronyms that promote understanding and implementation: GUIDE, CARE, and SPIN. In a consistent and clever manner these acronyms are used not only to present conceptual material relevant to all pertinent management topics, but also to present detailed examples and guidelines for practical use. Simonds has indeed served the management profession well by carefully crafting this brilliant volume. By weaving together this treasure chest of material, Simonds provides us with something new under the sun. I recommend this book highly, not only management students but also for experienced managers and leaders seeking to increase their effectiveness in working with employees."

-Ken Hultman, Ed.D. Author of the management classics:
Making Change Irresistible, and
Balancing Individual and Organizational Values
www.kenhultman.com

Achieving on Purpose:

Your
GUIDE
to
Managerial Success

by

Donald E. Simonds, M.Ed.

ISBN-13: 978-1497371729
ISBN-10: 1497371724

Cover design by Casey Ross
Author photograph by Simonds Photography

DEDICATION

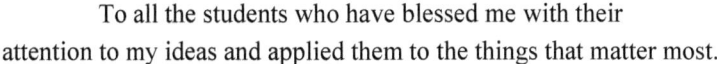

To all the students who have blessed me with their
attention to my ideas and applied them to the things that matter most.

Special thanks to Keith Akins and to Adyna Akins
for your friendship and encouragement to keep this project going.

ACKNOWLEDGEMENTS

My views on management have been influenced by many people throughout my lifetime, undoubtedly too many to mention individually. Allow me to acknowledge a few.

The late Jim Jeffries gave me my start in the training business. He was a wonderful mentor and I've tried to emulate his leadership style throughout my career.

All of my colleagues at The Coca-Cola Company Foods Division, Fluor E & C, SOHIO Petroleum Company, and Development Dimensions International added to that base of knowledge and made me a better instructor.

Alice Hoock hired me to teach in the Supervisory Management Certificate Program at Collin College. Over the past eight years, she has taken care of all the details, booked classrooms, requested necessary equipment, copied thousands of pages of handouts, and without her support this book would still be on the back burner.

Finally, the best for last, Sandy Simonds has proofed every page of everything I've ever written including this manuscript. She formatted this book and used her creativity to add the Section and Chapter design elements. Often she worked late into the evening, after a full day's work, postponing work on her own manuscript.

My heartfelt gratitude to all of you.

D. E. S.

Plano, TX
March, 2014
www.theentertrainerpro.com

CONTENTS

Section One - Fundamental Skills of Managing

Chapter 1   Introduction to the Management Process
            GUIDE/CARE/SPIN 1
Chapter 2   Planning Function 21
Chapter 3   Organizing Function 33
Chapter 4   Judgment 43

Section Two - Fundamental Skills of Communicating

Chapter 5   General Communication Concepts 53
Chapter 6   Formal Presentations 65
Chapter 7   Written Communication 75
Chapter 8   One to One Communication 81

Section Three - Selecting and Developing Organizational Talent

Chapter 9   Selecting Talent 89
Chapter 10 Orienting New Hires 109
Chapter 11 Training on Job Skills 117
Chapter 12 Developing Organizational Talent 123

Section Four - Directing Employees Toward Success

Chapter 13 Delegating 131
Chapter 14 Inspiring Desired Actions 139
Chapter 15 Coordinating Team Efforts 149
Chapter 16 Resolving Conflict 155

Section Five - Managing Change at Work

Chapter 17 System Theory 163

Chapter 18 Psychology of Habits and Attitudes 173

Chapter 19 Techniques of Group Process and Creative Thinking
            Methodology 177

Chapter 20 Project Management ....:........ 187

Section Six - Managing Performance

Chapter 21 Developing Performance Results Categories
            and Objectives 197

Chapter 22 Gaining Commitment to Performance Expectations 205

Chapter 23 Coaching and Reinforcing Performance 213

Chapter 24 Motivating Through Performance Review 223

Appendix A – Coaching Tips... 233

Appendix B – GUIDE Forms 237

Bibliography 245

Section One

Fundamental Skills
of Managing

1

Introduction to the Management Process
GUIDE / CARE / SPIN

———————————— ⵜ ————————————

INTRODUCTION

Conventional wisdom suggests that the fundamental functions of managing are Planning, Organizing, Leading, and Controlling. Furthermore, managers must Analyze Problems, Make Decisions, and Communicate continuously.

Within each of these functions, there are between three and six behavioral competencies. At the outset of each of the chapters in this book, I will define each of the behavioral competencies using a general definition and the list of key actions or behaviors that are required for that competency. On the following page is a list of the functions and the corresponding competencies.

For purposes of my training programs, I have chosen to split the leading function into two sub-functions called Staffing and Directing and I've combined Analyze Problems and Make Decisions into one competency called Judgment. This book follows my course outline for the Supervisory Management Certificate Series at Collin College.

To get the most out of this book, it might be useful for you to think of a situation in which there is a gap between where you are and where you want to be. The following is a short list of the kinds of situations to which you might apply the skills in this book:

Personal	Professional
Planning for retirement	Planning for a location move
Managing your household chores	Standardizing procedures
Organizing your wardrobe	Organizing a new department
Developing family duties	Developing position descriptions
Analyzing lifestyle choices	Analyzing equipment breakdowns
Making career decisions	Problem solving at work

———————————————————————————————————————

Fundamental Skills of Managing
Functions and Competencies

Sequential Functions:

1. Planning
2. Organizing
3. Staffing
4. Directing
5. Controlling

Continuous Functions:

1. Judgment
2. Communicating

Behavioral Competencies:

Planning

➢ Forecasting
➢ Setting Objectives
➢ Developing Strategies
➢ Budgeting
➢ Standardizing Procedures
➢ Developing Policies

Organizing

➢ Establishing Organization Structure
➢ Defining Job Qualifications
➢ Creating Position Descriptions

Staffing

➢ Selecting Talent
➢ Orienting New Hires
➢ Training on Job Skills
➢ Developing Organizational Talent

Directing

➢ Delegating
➢ Inspiring Desired Actions
➢ Coordinating Team Efforts
➢ Resolving Conflict
➢ Managing Change

Controlling

➢ Establishing Reporting Systems
➢ Developing Performance Standards
➢ Evaluating Results
➢ Taking Corrective Action
➢ Rewarding and Disciplining

Judgment

➢ Analyzing Problems
➢ Making Decisions
➢ Decisiveness

Communicating

➢ Selecting a Method
➢ Imparting a Message
➢ Receiving Feedback
➢ Making Corrections

Most human behavior is goal directed. People want to navigate successfully to goal achievement. They want to get from some current state of affairs to a desired state of affairs. In order to accomplish the goal they need to understand where they are, where they are going and an acceptable way to get there.

I begin each series with introductions during which I ask the participants to describe their best and worst managers. Here is a list of the most typical responses:

Best Manager	Worst Manager
• Expected me to solve problems	• Task oriented
• Trusted me	• Lacked trust
• Encouraged upward feedback	• Ineffective communicator
• Provided support	• Controlling
• Solicited my ideas	• Micromanaged
• Listened	• Overlooked bad behavior
• Delegated tasks	• Eavesdropped
• Connected on a personal level	• Focused only on my weak points
• Provided constructive feedback	• Disciplined in public
• Believed in my capabilities	• Showed no respect
• Was open to new ideas	• Had conflicting goals
• Praised me	• Lied to make herself look good
• Mentor to me	• Late to work

As you can see, people think fondly of managers who treat them with respect and are frustrated with managers who seem to be driven only by the task at hand. Let's look at the historical context of this. Then you can compare your thoughts to those of the experts.

Here are some of the highlights:

1924 – Hawthorne Effect

Efficiency experts at Western Electric in Hawthorne, Illinois were hired to explore, among other things, the effect of increasing illumination in the plant. The assumption being that the output of the workers would increase if the lighting improved.

Two groups were involved; an experimental group and a control group. Researchers increased the amount of light when dealing with the experimental group. As you might imagine, productivity went up. When dealing with the control group they did nothing but observe. Surprisingly, productivity went up.

The conclusion known as the Hawthorne Effect can be summarized like this; when people know their behavior is being monitored, they will change their behavior to create a favorable impression. In other words, if people don't do what you *expect*, they will do what you *inspect*.

1954 – Maslow's Hierarchy of Needs

I actually believe that managers cannot motivate employees. You can't motivate me and I can't motivate you. You motivate you and I motivate me. Abraham Maslow described a hierarchy of needs which must be fulfilled in order for people to motivate themselves. Here is the hierarchy, but you should read it from the bottom up. Simply stated, a person is motivated by physiological needs first and will not move up the ladder to safety needs until those physiological needs are met. Subsequently, a person's social needs are not important until the safety needs are met and so forth up the ladder.

> **Self-actualization** – needs are met when a person reaches the highest level of competence and feels the joy of achievement. A politician self-actualizes when elected to the office he seeks. A writer self-actualizes when her novel is published.

> **Esteem** – needs are met when a person is given recognition by others. This can happen in a corporation when an individual complements another or when the company promotes the person to a position of higher authority.

> **Social** - needs are met when a person feels a sense of belonging or acceptance in the company. People search out others who have the same beliefs and those who will affirm them.

> **Safety** - needs are met when a person feels a sense of security. I want to remain free of the hazards of life. In business, I want to know I won't get fired; my pension won't be stolen, etc.

> **Physiological** - needs are met when a person has shelter, food, clothing, etc. I won't be able to concentrate on my work, if I'm starving.

I am frequently asked about money as a motivator. Now money can play a role in all of these, but when people ask for more money there is probably a reason rooted in one of the personal needs listed above. When people ask for more money you should find out how they want to spend it. For example, if I want more money so I can buy a boat. Then, my motivation is probably either social or esteem. Knowing the personal motivators for an individual can help a leader decide how to treat that person.

Many years ago a research study indicated that a raise in pay motivated employees on average for nine days. So, if you think you can motivate people with money you will have to give them a raise every nine days. And I suspect that if you did that, sooner or later, the raises would have to come at more frequent intervals. There will be more on money, in the section on Frederick Herzberg.

1960 – Douglas McGregor (Chris Argyris 1971 – Behavior Patterns)

You've probably heard of Douglas McGregor. He described Theory X – Theory Y in his classic work *The Human Side of Enterprise*. Theory X and Y are attitudes or predispositions toward people. They are not right or wrong, but do lead to managerial behavior patterns.

The patterns could be summarized as follows:

Theory X	Theory Y
• Task Driven	• Relationship Driven
• Close Supervision	• Open to Experimentation
• Not Open to Feelings	• Supportive
• High Structure	• Facilitating

Consequently, Theory X managers are perceived to be like the way my students described their worst managers and Theory Y managers are perceived to be like the way my students described their best managers.

1959 – Frederick Herzberg

In his *The Motivation to Work*, Herzberg described two sets of factors he called motivators and hygiene factors. He claimed that those things that motivate us come from the job itself not from the company or from supervision.

Notice where money is on the following chart:

Motivators	Hygiene Factors
The Job Itself	Environment
• Achievement	• Policies and Administration
• Recognition for Accomplishments	• Supervision
• Challenging Work	• Working Conditions
• Increased Responsibility	• Interpersonal Relations
• Growth and Development	• Money, Status, Security

The motivators cause the employee to want to work and are the equivalent of Theory Y behaviors. The hygiene factors may be necessary, but companies should provide for them and then shut up about them. They are the most likely cause of dissatisfaction in organizations. Indeed, the worst thing an organization can do is to provide a hygiene factor and then take it away. For instance, offering ten paid holidays annually and then changing the policy to eight paid holidays could cause a major uproar among the troops.

1964 – Blake & Mouton – Managerial Grid

In the following graphic, you'll notice that Robert Blake and Jane Mouton implied that someone with a high concern for people and a high concern for task accomplishment would make the best leader. While the other extremes have negative connotations, they may be desirable under the right circumstances.

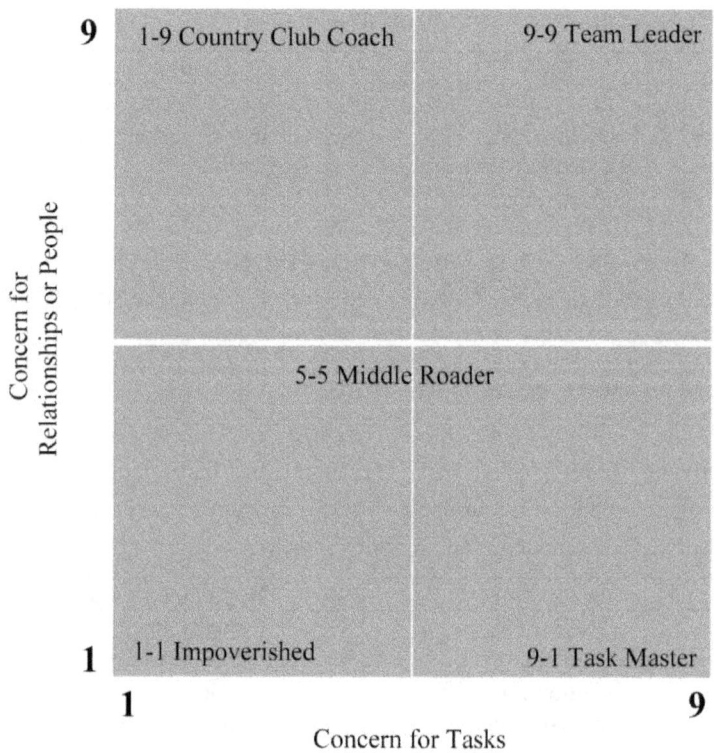

Assume you are on an airplane preparing to land at LAX when it begins to pitch violently, and the pilot's voice is heard over the intercom system. In a rather calm voice he says, "Ladies and Gentlemen the plane is experiencing intense backwash from the jet engines in front of us. Does anyone have any ideas on what to do about this problem?"

If I were a passenger on that airliner, the last thing I would want is for the pilot to use a participative leadership style. I would want him to do what needs to be done and tell me what to do and how to do it to survive. In short, it would be desirable for him to be a task master.

Likewise, there may be situations when a leader should change behavior to fit the need at hand. This is what led Paul Hersey and Ken Blanchard to their model.

1969 – Hersey & Blanchard – Situational Leadership

Basically what Hersey and Blanchard felt was missing from the Blake and Mouton model was the employee's level of maturity. That is how willing and able the employees are to take responsibility for their own behavior. The following diagram portrays the leader's style changing as the employee's maturity changes.

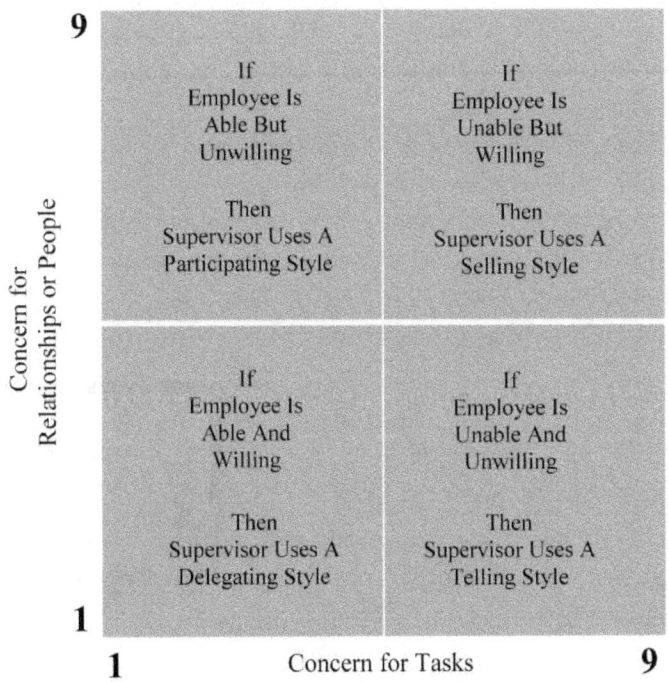

Maturity level has nothing to do with chronological age. A person could be an M1 if new in the job and not feeling confident or competent. For example, when I took my first sales job I had never sold anything in my life; therefore, I appreciated my boss telling me what to do, how to do it, and when. As I gained some success, my willingness to take on the responsibility increased but my ability was still low; so, I appreciated my boss using a different style to influence my decisions.

When a person is clearly in the M3 category, the effective leader should use a participating style to increase the employee's willingness to assume responsibility.

Finally, the delegating style is used when the employee is performing at a high level. The leader may simply state the objectives of the task and allow the employee to figure out how, when, and what is necessary.

2002 – Simonds and Akins – GUIDE, CARE, & SPIN

We believe that both task-relevant behavior and relationship-relevant behavior should be used in all dealings with an employee. We developed three models using acronyms that would make it easy to memorize. These mnemonic devises are GUIDE, CARE, & SPIN.

GUIDE provides a repeatable process for people to follow that maximizes their likelihood of a successful outcome. GUIDE draws a task-relevant map.

People also want to feel respected and valued—that other people care about them and want them to succeed.

As a successful manager, you pay close attention to the needs of the people you are managing. In every assignment there is a task to be done and a relationship to be built or preserved. It is up to you to ensure that both are handled effectively.

GUIDE is your "Task Map." It gives you the steps to follow to ensure that you are accomplishing the task part of the assignment. It helps you navigate to accomplish the task at hand. The key steps to GUIDE are:

Gather information

Understand the available information

Investigate alternatives

Decide on the best course of action,
    Develop a plan, and **D**o it

Evaluate progress and results, **E**xpress gratitude

> At times
> **G** can stand for Give information and
> **D** can stand for Deliver the service

Take CARE of the Relationship

GUIDE is essentially a problem-solving and decision-making model that can be applied in virtually any situation requiring a move from the current state of affairs to a desired state of affairs.

Interacting effectively with others includes caring for them. CARE is a set of "Relationship Building" behaviors:

Commit - Giving and expecting dedication builds trust and involvement.

Affirm - Showing acceptance of the individual as a person preserves esteem and a sense of security in the journey.

Recognize - Praising a person's value, effort, contributions, or results builds esteem and confidence.

Empathize - Demonstrating that you are listening shows that you understand the person's message and feelings.

Together GUIDE and CARE help people successfully accomplish tasks in the context of positive, trusting, and reinforcing relationships.

Put the Right SPIN on Feedback

Virtually every managing situation requires giving feedback. Without feedback very little learning takes place. Feedback need not be complex, but it does need to be complete. SPIN assures that your feedback contains all of the necessary information to be understood and effective.

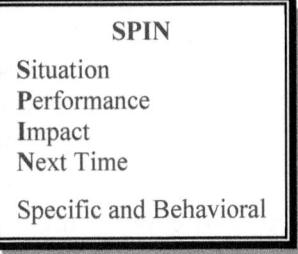

SPIN

Situation
Performance
Impact
Next Time

Specific and Behavioral

The most effective feedback is specific, sincere, and behavioral. Without those characteristics, feedback creates defensiveness or is ignored.

SPIN is a model for keeping feedback specific and behavioral. Use CARE as you SPIN. That will protect the relationship during feedback.

Using GUIDE, CARE, and SPIN will dramatically increase the probability of success for you and your direct reports.

GUIDE

Using GUIDE helps keep you focused on the task part of your job. It ensures that you clarify the objective of the undertaking and maintain focus as you proceed to the desired outcome. What follows is a more detailed description of each component of the GUIDE model.

Gather Information

The first step in tackling any task or challenge is to gather as much information as you can about the situation. Seems pretty obvious doesn't it? Yet so many times the results hoped for aren't achieved because of a failure to gather the right information. Notice I did not say *all* the information. I said the *right* information. Trying to gather all the information can lead to frustrated associates, unnecessary delays and analysis paralysis.

GUIDE can be adapted to any situation in which there is a gap between the current state and a desired state. The problem should be framed in those terms.

Gathering information takes on many forms depending upon the context, but could include:

> Asking Questions (orally or in writing)
> Listening
> Observing (paying attention)
> Sensing (seeing, hearing, touching, smelling and tasting)
> Reading (books, magazines, signs, web pages)

In the simplest sense, gathering the following types of information helps to take more effective action:

1. What is the current situation?
2. What is the desired situation?
3. Desired state minus current state equals the gap.
4. What resources are available to get from the current to the desired situation?

> Time
> People (expertise, motivation, involvement, talent, muscle)
> Money
> Space
> Tools
> Supplies

Understand the Available Information

Anyone who has asked for one thing and received another realizes the importance of ensuring understanding. In fast food restaurants it's as simple as getting a small soft drink when you really wanted a large. It happens when a real estate agent shows inappropriate property to a prospective buyer; even when good matches are out there. Gathering information and then not checking to ensure understanding leads to more missed opportunities and unrealized goals than any other cause.

Ensuring understanding means everyone involved in the situation shares the same interpretation. "Everyone" means the buyer and the seller, both parties to the negotiation, both you and the person you are managing.

Three techniques to check the information include:

➢ Repeating or summarizing the information
➢ Checking for agreement on the details
➢ Asking others to state their understanding and comparing it to yours

As with gathering information, ensuring understanding is not something you do once.

As you get additional information and formulate new ideas, you should cycle back and check again.

At the conclusion of this step, everyone involved should have a clear understanding of the current state, the desired state, and therefore, the gap.

Investigate Alternatives

Life would be simple, if not boring, if every problem had one, and only one, solution; the journey would be unchallenging if every destination had only one path to get there. Life is full of choices. In fact, choices are what life is all about.

Sometimes the best solution is simply to change the way you are thinking about the current state or the desired state. At other times, you actually need to do things to bring about the change you desire. It is important to decide the best option. As a transition into this step, it might be wise to revisit the situation and *reframe* it. At the very least, state the desired outcome of this decision.

To be sure, there are times when the choices are very limited or when there really is only one right answer. In those situations, you may be better off simply offering the alternatives and moving to the next step in GUIDE.

However, not knowing the alternatives is rarely a good thing. If you have limited time or if the probable list of alternatives is small, seek ideas first and offer ideas second.

On the other hand, too many alternatives can lead to analysis paralysis and unnecessary confusion.

Investigating alternatives includes two elements:

> Choosing a developmental thinking method, and
> Generating a list of alternatives.

GUIDE offers various techniques and tools for generating alternatives. The techniques used to generate alternatives will depend on the context of the situation.

Brainstorming: Generate a list of ideas without evaluating the ideas initially.

Movie Magic: Go in your mind to a favorite vacation spot and create dialogue with the locals asking for solution ideas to your problem.

Animation Exercise: Animation means to give life or motion to. Ask someone to "become" the MRI equipment and describe solutions from the machine's perspective.

Preferences: Look at options for solving a problem and ask, "Which do you prefer a steel casing or aluminum?"

Force Field Analysis: Examine the forces that are "contributing to" or "hindering" a solution and then develop ways of removing or reducing the restraining forces.

Features and Benefits: Focus on the problem as given and ask, "How can I make the features more beneficial?" (i.e. lighter, faster, stronger, cheaper, and more efficient?)

There are hundreds of creative techniques for generating alternatives. I will name and describe others later in Chapter 19.

*D*ecide on the Best course of Action, *D*evelop a Plan, and *D*o It

Nothing ever gets done until you decide on what you are going to do and do it. If the situation is very complex, filled with uncertainty or rife with conflict, making the decision can be very difficult. Once you and your associate have generated sufficient information and developed a common understanding, you need to decide what to do and either develop a plan or simply do it.

The Decide step includes:

> Reducing the list to a set of reasonable, viable alternatives
> Choosing the most viable alternative
> Developing a plan, and doing it

GUIDE offers various techniques and tools for reducing alternatives. The techniques used to reduce the list will depend on the context of the situation.

Stakeholder Analysis: Discuss who will be affected by the decision and identify needs and preferences.

Win-Win: Select those solutions that would satisfy everyone's basic needs.

Must Haves, Nice to Haves: Identify aspects of the solution that are required and those that are desired. Reduce the list to alternatives that *may* offer both.

SOP: Consider whether Standard Operating Procedures offer a reasonable alternative. Although they might feel restrictive, most are there for valid reasons.

GUIDE offers various methods for making decisions such as:

- Pain vs. Gain
- Must Haves, Nice to Haves and Weighted Alternatives
- Return on Investment
- Choosing From a List of Winners
- Balancing Long and Short Term Consequences
- What's in My Control? What's Not?
- Seeking Win-Win Outcomes

No one has a crystal ball. But the goal is to *simplify complexity*, *reduce uncertainty* and *resolve conflict* which leads to better decisions.

Evaluate Progress and Results, Express Gratitude

It is hard to celebrate victory until you know victory has been achieved. Likewise, it is hard to get back on track unless you know you are off track to begin with.

Evaluating progress and results may be simple or involved, again depending on the situation. The desired outcome is the standard. If the desired outcome is customers who are satisfied because they have the right food and were treated with respect while being served, then a simple question and answer confirms the results. For example, "May I help you with anything else?" followed by "Thanks for coming in. Let me know if I can help you with anything else."

More complex situations require more sophisticated measurement methods. Many decisions take time to be proven out. Some decisions require input from multiple people and sources.

For example:

> ➢ How do you know you are making good hiring decisions?
> ➢ How do you know that a capital investment is yielding the desired return?
> ➢ How do you know that a negotiated agreement optimized the outcome for all parties?
> ➢ How do you know that a direct report benefited from your coaching?

Evaluating progress and results enables you to correct mistakes and confirm success. Expressing gratitude acknowledges contributions and ceremoniously brings the GUIDE journey to an end.

Evaluating progress and Expressing gratitude includes:

> ➢ Measuring outcomes relative to desired outcomes
> ➢ Confirming satisfaction
> ➢ Thanking those involved

CARE

Using GUIDE alone does not guarantee a positive outcome. Many situations can be tense and emotional for both parties - especially for the person being managed. Effective leaders work hard to manage the relationship during interactions. The relationship is as important as the task.

CARE gives you a model of effective relationship skills. Using CARE helps to reduce barriers, resistance, and tension that can arise during interventions, while encouraging participation.

Commit

Giving and expecting commitment builds trust and involvement. Involving people in identifying alternatives and making decisions builds their commitment to the journey ahead. Simple statements or questions encourage involvement. Examples include:

> ➢ What ideas do you have for _____?
> ➢ What role do you see yourself taking in _____?
> ➢ I need your help with _____.

Declaring commitment in specific and sincere terms builds confidence and trust. Examples include:

> ➢ Let me know how I can help you with _____.
> ➢ I am committed to seeing you succeed with ___.
> ➢ This is important to us and I will help you in any way I can to finish _____.
> ➢ I will delay X to focus on Y with you _____.
> ➢ I will be right there with you when you _____.

Showing your commitment does not mean taking over and doing tasks for others. It means being very clear about how you will support them as they strive to achieve challenging goals or to improve their performance in some way.

Affirm

Affirming another person is something you can do in every single interaction. But what exactly does affirm mean?

The dictionary defines affirm as:

1. to declare positively; assert 2. to confirm; ratify

In the context of CARE you are affirming the *value of the person*. You are showing that you accept the person for whom he or she is. You value that person as a fellow human being.

Affirming the value of the individual as a person preserves self-esteem, status, and a sense of security. People's sense of self-worth dramatically affects how they respond in specific situations, especially in important situations that require them to interact with others. Examples of situations in which self-esteem and confidence are particularly vulnerable are:

> Being an applicant in an interview,
> Negotiating for almost anything,
> Trying something new,
> Receiving feedback on either effective, or ineffective performance,
> Working with others to solve a problem or improve a situation,
> Seeking almost any kind of service or trying to get poor service corrected, and
> Working through a conflict.

Saying things that affirm them as valued individuals helps to maintain self-esteem during the interaction and helps to keep the conversation positive and productive. The most effective affirmations are *specific* and *sincere*.

Examples in specific contexts might include:

> "It sounds like you did everything you could do to resolve that situation."
> "I appreciate your keeping things going under such difficult circumstances."
> "It means a lot to me that you are willing to offer creative options to help both sides get what each need."
> "That is a really interesting idea."

Affirmation of the person is particularly helpful during awkward or potentially embarrassing moments. But it does not have to be restricted to challenging, difficult interactions or to even specific situations. You can affirm the value of someone many times and many ways.

> Sincerity is the defining characteristic of effective affirmation.
>
> Bottom line: If you cannot be sincere ... do not affirm!

For example you can say:

> "I am really glad you're here today."
> "I always appreciate your positive approach to things."
> "I know I can count on you. You always give it your best effort."
> "I am so glad you are on our team."

Sincere affirmation has a powerful and positive effect on relationships. Insincere affirmation can have the opposite effect. It probably will be seen as sarcastic and it sends a signal that you do not really affirm the person's value.

Recognize

Recognizing a person's contributions or results builds esteem and confidence.

When people are recognized for their inputs, they become more assured and confident of their status. They know where they stand and are more likely to enjoy where they are standing. Sincere compliments and recognition for accomplishments are primary ways to show respect for someone.

Recognition and Affirmation are similar. The key difference is that recognition is for a specific accomplishment, input, effort, event, etc.; whereas, affirmation is for specific ways that you value the person. Examples of "Recognize" include:

> "Congratulations on winning the quality award. That helps accomplish your vendor of choice goal."

> "I am very impressed by how well you handled that unhappy customer. When you said you were sorry she was so apprehensive, you were able to get to the heart of her complaint."

Empathize

When people are in potentially threatening situations, there is a risk of strong agitation of feelings such as sorrow, fear, hate, etc., getting in the way. One of the effective methods of avoiding or diffusing interfering emotions is to empathize, to show that you understand how the person feels about a specific issue or situation.

Empathy is not sympathy or apathy. It is not feeling sorry for someone. Rather it is trying to see the situation from the other person's perspective.

Having empathy and showing empathy are not the same things either. Showing empathy is an active step that helps reduce tension and lower resistance. It is saying things about the specifics of the situation and the feelings the person is likely to have in the situation.

> Empathy addresses the:
> **Situation**
> and the
> **Emotion**

Examples include:

> ➤ "I can see how being stuck in traffic and being late to work would be very frustrating."
> ➤ "You must be really excited about winning the quality award."
> ➤ "Not knowing what the final cost will be must be a bit unnerving."

By empathizing, you show that you are listening carefully to the person's situation and feelings.

Put the Right SPIN on Feedback

The most effective feedback is both *specific* and *behavioral*. It also provides guidance for the next time the person faces a similar situation. Specific behaviors have three key components: Situation, Performance and Impact.

Situation

Every action takes place in some context or situation. It is the situation that helps us understand why people do what they do. When describing the situation keep it very specific. Situation describes:

- Who
- What
- Where
- When
- How

Collectively they shed light on the question of *why*.

Performance

When people behave, they do something. Generally, a person's performance is observable. It takes place in time and space. The most effective feedback describes actual behavior. That means quoting what someone said or describing what someone did.

During feedback, performance statements sound like the following:

- You said, "_____."
- You did _____.
- You asked, "_____?"

Impact

Impact is the effect of the person's action on the specific situation. It explains what difference the person's performance made. Impact helps summarize the effectiveness of the performance. Examples of statements that describe impact include:

- "They were delighted with the quality of your work and wrote a letter praising it."
- "Volunteering for that task eased everyone else's burden and ensured that we could get the project done on time."
- "Coming in late, or not showing up at all, makes it hard on others who have to fill in for you. It hurts your reputation too."

These describe *how much* the performance helped or hindered the situation.

Next Time

Whether the person's performance had a positive or negative impact, it helps to suggest what to do next time. If the performance was positive, you might say:

> ➤ "Keep it up. It paid off this time and it will pay off *next time* too."
> ➤ "It would be great if you handled the situation the same way *next time.*"
> ➤ "You will continue to have a great impact if you handle it the same way *next time.*"
> ➤ "That strategy works for you. Do it again!"

These *reinforce* the positive performance.

It is particularly important to offer suggestions for next time when the impact of the person's performance was not effective. Offering alternative performance strategies will help the person see the difference between what he did, and what he could have done to be more effective.

When you suggest a different performance strategy for next time, it helps to explain your rationale. Tell the person why the alternative might be more effective.

Examples:

> ➤ "Next time you could ask John for help. Then he would probably feel more involved in solving the problem."
> ➤ "Next time call before you go there. That way you can save yourself a lot of time and aggravation of no one being there when you arrive."
> ➤ "Next time you are in heavy traffic, try putting plenty of space between you and the car in front of you, especially if the person behind isn't. That will reduce the chance of being forced into an accident."

These help to *encourage* a change of behavior.

Positive feedback and feedback for improvement are both important for growth and development. Balancing the two promote development and preserve self-esteem. Taking CARE when giving feedback preserves the quality of the relationship.

2

Planning Function

INTRODUCTION

The Planning Function is the first of the sequential functions. This chapter covers the following behavioral competencies:

Forecasting – Analyzing current and historical data to determine future trends. These might include:

- ➤ Predicting new markets, products or services
- ➤ Anticipating delivery schedules to reduce excess inventory
- ➤ Projecting resource needs (materials, facilities, energy)
- ➤ Foreseeing labor or succession requirements

Setting Objectives – Describing concrete outcomes related to goals of the organization.

- ➤ Specific, Measurable, Attainable, Realistic, Time bound
- ➤ Example – "To reduce turnover by 50% within 12 months"

Developing Strategies – Outlining the formal consideration of an organization's future course. This vision should include the answers to the following:

1. "What do we do?"
2. "For whom do we do it?"
3. "How do we excel?"

Budgeting – Allocating financial resources based upon logical assumptions, facts and guidelines with regard to your intended strategies.

- ➤ Analyzing previous budgets
- ➤ Considering project requirements
- ➤ Requesting vendor quotations
- ➤ Allowing for contingencies

Standardizing Procedures – Documenting all steps and activities of a process to ensure a quality product or service.

> Installing changes permanently
> Establishing a maintenance schedule
> Building it into the cultural system

Developing Policies – Guiding decisions which achieve rational outcomes. They should include the following components:

1. A purpose statement
2. An applicability and scope statement
3. An effective date
4. A responsibilities section
5. The specific regulations

Let's explore the use of GUIDE within the context of planning. Assume that your Chief Executive Officer has asked you to prepare a plan to move the office from Dallas to Ft. Worth where the rent is cheaper.

Gather Information

Remember, gathering information means looking at what has happened historically. You might ask questions like:

> "What do we know?"
> "Has this happened before?"
> "Is there documentation of a previous plan in this area?"
> "Why is this a problem or responsibility for me?"

In the context of the plan to move the corporate office, I want to know if we have ever moved before. If so, did we use a moving company? Was the move successful? If not, why not? It's important to look at what has happened before so we can repeat our previous successes and correct anything that went wrong. I also want to know what went wrong and how severe the impact was.

Understand the Available Information

This step is about verifying what you know. You might want to ask yourself:

> "Who could I call?"
> "Who would know about previous plans in this area?"
> "Who could verify my facts?"

Based upon what you know and have verified, state your objective. What MUST happen? The object should be written in specific, measurable terms (see the competency for Setting Objectives later in this Chapter) such as, "To complete the move of all Dallas-based employees to the Ft. Worth location by Labor Day."

Investigate Alternatives

The future starts here. In exploring alternatives, anything goes. This is the most fun step because you can be creative. The purpose of this step is to create a list of alternatives for all aspects of the plan. You might ask:

> ➤ What are the possible activities to accomplish the MUST?
> ➤ Who could do it?
> ➤ Who should do it?
> ➤ When is it possible?

Before moving into the Decide step, make sure you have exhausted all possibilities.

Decide on the Best Course of Action, Develop a Plan, and Do It

This is the plan. List all action steps in chronological order. One of the best ways to do this is to work backwards from the established completion date. You might develop a flow chart starting on the far right with the deadline. Then ask yourself, "What has to happen just before that to meet the deadline?" Then, "What needs to happen before that?" and "Before that?" etc. until you have completed all necessary steps.

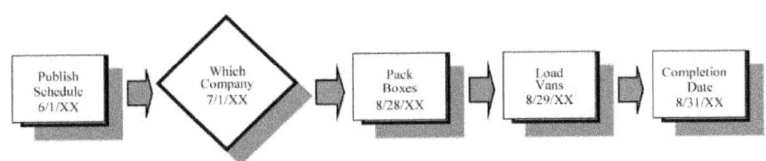

Then assign responsibility for each step to the appropriate person. Make a list of all resources available for each step. Consider any raw materials, facilities, money, energy, and additional labor that might be needed for each step.

A critical review at this stage is important. There may be potential risks for which contingencies need to be developed. Ask yourself, "What could go wrong?" or, "Where might there be decision delays, bottlenecks, redundancies, etc.?"

Next, you will want to differentiate between small and high risk. This can be done by determining the probability of the potential problem occurring and assessing the magnitude of the adverse consequences should the potential problem occur. You might ask yourself, "What is the likelihood that this problem will actually happen?" and, "If it does happen, will the impact be severe?"

Then develop contingencies for those possibilities, especially the ones that have a high probability of occurrence or would be very costly in regard to time or money.

Finally, publish the plan in the form of a project Gantt chart which is a bar graph showing the potential start dates, duration, and overlap of tasks which can be done simultaneously. See the following form for an example. Inform all those involved and provide a copy of the plan.

*E*valuate Progress and Results, *E*xpress Gratitude

You will evaluate the results after the plan has been executed. The evaluation will determine what went well and what could have been done better and how. It is appropriate to document the results for continuous improvement purposes.

Finally, thank those involved for the things they did that led to a successful move.

PROJECT MANAGEMENT PLANNING FORM

Define The Problem Or Opportunity: *Move the company offices to Ft. Worth by Labor Day*

TASKS	Raw Materials	Facilities	Energy	Labor	Money	Drop Dead Date	MONTHLY SCHEDULE June – July – August
1. Publish Preliminary Moving Schedule	Paper		Electric	Dave		6/1/2012	
2. Explore Moving Companies		Room # 222		Team		7/1/2012	
3. Arrange for Utilities		Office	Phone	Bob		6/15/2012	
4. Change Address on all Stationery	Stationery			Supplier	Budget $	7/1/2012	
5. Evaluate What Will Go or Not Go				Team		7/1/2012	
6. Order Moving Materials		Shredder	Electric	Team		8/1/2012	
7. Shred Files Not Going	Boxes, Tape, Etc.	Storage Room		B J & L	Budget $	8/1/2012	
8. Pack Moving Boxes				Team		8/28/2012	
9. Notify Customers, Vendors, Etc. of Move	Stationery			Team		8/1/2012	
10. Request Mail Forwarding				Dave		8/1/2012	
11. Send Press Release	Stationery			P. R.		8/1/2012	
12. Ensure New Location is Ready				Team		8/27/2012	
13. Load Moving Vans				Movers		8/29/2012	
14. Deliver & Set-up New Office			Electric	All		8/31/2012	
15. Clean Old Property & Leave Keys	Party Supplies			Crew		8/31/2012	
16. Celebrate	Forms			Dave		Happy Labor Day	
17. Document Results						9/5/2012	

CONTINGENCIES: *If cost runs over $10,000 – document potential ROI & get approval.*

The previous plan is based upon the assumption that a lease for a new office location has already been signed. Otherwise there might be additional items in the plan that could start at least six-months out. These might include researching various properties, negotiating a lease agreement, applying for permits, cleaning or remodeling the space, etc.

You may also think of more steps in the plan. Those listed are minimal for illustrative purposes.

Applying GUIDE to the Planning Competencies

Let's take a look at how the use of GUIDE might be different when applied to the various competencies in the planning realm?

Forecasting

Forecasting is the most difficult of the thirty behavioral competencies of managing. Quite simply, Forecasting is looking into the future. It requires guessing at what the world will be like in the coming year or longer.

In Gathering information, one might survey customers, vendors, or industry experts about the projected needs for products or services. One might do a trend analysis to project resource needs for materials, facilities, or labor. Finally, one might conduct a cause-effect analysis to predict new markets or an increase in sales six months in the future.

The problem with these methods is that they are unreliable. Nobody really knows what will happen. That doesn't mean you shouldn't forecast, but when you get to the Decide step a stronger emphasis should be placed on contingency planning.

A classic example of what can go wrong happened when I was working with Fluor E & C in Houston. I worked for Fluor from February, 1981 to June, 1983. During my first year the business was booming. Fluor executives offered incentives to employees for recruiting friends and business associates to come join the ever expanding troops.

The building we were in was overflowing into satellite offices and, at the time, we had a little over four thousand employees. The executives predicted that the oil business was going to continue booming and that we needed a larger space. They projected we would need to grow to ten thousand employees within the next five years to keep up with the increasing business.

They put five million dollars down on a piece of property in Sugarland, Texas. They hired an architectural firm to design a new, five-pod, high tech facility and we all began participating in the development of the design. It was very exciting because we were asked to think out of the box, picture the best equipment, and prepare a state-of-the-art facility for our business.

In 1982, Fluor sold the building we were in to Aramco and agreed to vacate the building by1984. Unfortunately, within about six months of all this fury the oil companies announced they would not be building any more processing plants and Fluor's business began to crumble.

Instead of growing to 10,000 employees, the company started lay-offs. I was cut at about the 1,800 mark and eventually 800 employees moved into the first pod of the new building.

Why? Because nobody knows for sure what the future holds.

Setting Objectives

To achieve the best results with your work, it will be important to define your work in terms of goals and objectives. Typically, I start with a statement of need. This should be a phrase or short sentence. For example, "To resolve all customer inquiries within 36 hours and to the satisfaction of the customer and me."

Next, you'll want to test your need statement against the following SMART criteria:

-Specific -Measurable -Attainable -Realistic -Time bound

Specific goals are defined in terms of quality, quantity, timeliness and cost. Here are some examples of measurement methods for any job:

Area of Measurement	Methods
Quality	* Number of specifications met * % Error rate * % Scrap * Number of complaints received
Quantity	* Number of units produced * Number of units run * Number of calls taken * Sales revenue generated
Timeliness	* % Scheduled dates met * Number of deadlines met * % Within specified timeframes
Cost	* Dollars spent * % Within budget * Dollars of overtime cost

Measurable goals have defined the optimal level. For instance, to produce $500,000 in sales in 12 months is a measurable goal. To improve the image of the organization is not.

Any goal that requires somebody to change behavior or improve productivity must be Attainable. Obviously, if the request is beyond the capacity of the people involved, it's not going to get done. It's important to consider not only your ability but also your willingness to make the change. If both ability and willingness are there, then the goal is attainable.

Realistic goals are attainable under the current circumstances. You might ask yourself if the goal is attainable under the current budget or other economic constraints of the organization. Is the goal attainable given organizational policy and does it tie into the goals of the department in which you work? Is it realistic to assume you can do the work, given your job description, without usurping the authority of some other person?

Time bound means that the goal has clock or calendar constraints. Some goals can be completed within a matter of minutes; others may require a calendar or fiscal year.

In addition to the SMART criteria, your goals should be both challenging and rewarding. Challenging goals require optimal effort on your part. It is inappropriate to have goals that are too easy or too hard. In either extreme, the result is demoralizing. You will rise to the occasion if challenged but won't do well if you feel overwhelmed.

Rewarding goals are ones that incorporate the benefit of accomplishing them. For instance, "If I can figure out a way to get XYZ Company to send its people to us, I'll have a crack at that new assignment I've been after."

The following goal statement meets the criteria that's just been established, "To resolve all customer inquiries within 36 hours and to the satisfaction of the customer and me."

Developing Strategies

A strategy usually applies to a conceptual guideline for the way a company will do business. It can be a statement as to how the company will differentiate itself from competitors or how it will excel in the marketplace.

For example, let's say I want to start an Art Studio. Here are three strategies for running the business:

1. Create my own original art and sell it through my website
2. Purchase third party art at wholesale and resell through my website
3. Establish low prices by mass producing art from my originals

---

Budgeting

Not unlike forecasting, using GUIDE here means:

➢ Gathering information regarding previous budgets
➢ Considering how your current situation might change things
➢ Requesting bids from vendors, if necessary
➢ Building in contingencies

Unless this is a zero-based budget, the easiest way to complete the annual budget is to take last year's budget and add enough to cover the current inflation rate.

Standardizing Procedures

Standardizing procedures, aka Standard Operating Procedures (SOP), means documenting the step-by-step activities of a process to ensure a quality product or service. This is particularly important when working on a continuous improvement project. The steps must be explicitly explained, so an employee could follow them, complete the operation accurately, and meet the required performance expectations.

Once the new process has been tested and proven to work at the desired level of quality, it's important to install the change permanently. By preparing the SOP, including a narrative and process map, employees will be able to complete their tasks effectively. Conduct training on the procedure and have each employee sign the procedure manual indicating the training was completed and showing a commitment to follow the procedure without exception.

Just as you might conduct preventative maintenance on your equipment, it is a good idea to establish a maintenance schedule for SOPs. This might include conducting quarterly reviews of those employees who are using the procedure to ensure its being followed as intended. If people are taking short-cuts, then refresher training is in order.

Finally, build the procedures into the culture system. Establish a Champion, someone from executive management who promotes the SOP by communicating the importance of following the procedure and models the use of the SOP. Include the SOP in company value statements. Create posters with SOP slogans that can be seen in hallways, cafeteria, etc. Reward people who follow the SOP. Discuss the use of SOP during staff meetings as a regular agenda item.

Developing Policies

In large corporations these are probably already developed. Your only task is to get a copy of the policy manual and review it so you can administer the policies.

It's important that you understand the policies, but not hide behind them. Don't tell an employee that the reason your taking action is that the policy says you must. Rather state the policy and add, "I agree with this policy and as a leader in this company I have an obligation to enforce it. These policies were developed for a reason...." And, if necessary, explain the rationale behind the policy, so the employee understands it.

Many policies are written to ensure that a company abides by obligatory regulations, like the EEOC guidelines for fair and equal treatment from the first employment interview through separation. Other policies may be for the benefit of clients; such as, a store's return policy. In any event, policies are written for a valid reason, usually to guide decision-making in a generally accepted business practice.

In a small organization, policies may not be developed. I worked for three major corporations after college. Each had over 30,000 employees. Then I joined a company with fewer than 200 employees. One day I called a vice president and asked about a policy and he said, "We don't have one." This shocked me to the bones and I said, "We don't?" Then he said, "No, we make decisions around here. Tell me what you want to do."

I loved that about small companies and consequently feel more suited to be with a small organization. Therefore, I recommend that if you are in a small company that you make decisions not policies until the need arises.

When the time comes, written policies should include the following components:

1. A purpose statement – This is the rationale for the policy and the desired outcome if applied.

2. An applicability and scope statement – This describes the target audience; including, who it includes, who it excludes, and what actions will be taken. This statement should help avoid any unintended consequences.

3. An effective date – This indicates when the policy comes into force.

4. A responsibilities section – This area would outline who has the authority to administer or enforce the policy. For example, the Human Resources department might be assigned policies that involve hiring and firing decisions. As would be the case for a policy to promote from within.

5. The specific regulation – This section includes the explicit rule and consequences of violating the rule. For instance, one company may state that disciplinary action requires that the

employee be suspended without pay for three days. In another, the same offense might require a two-day "decision making leave" during which time the employee is paid but he must make a decision of whether he wants to work for the company or not.

Planning GUIDE

 **G**ather information
Who, what, where, how, when, why regarding history of plans in this area

> Commit
> Affirm
> Recognize
> Empathize

Understand the available information
Check for understanding, who would know?

Investigate alternatives
List all possible activities based upon what MUST happen. Who could/should do it? When is it possible?

Decide on the best course of action, Develop a plan, and Do it
Finalize action steps in chronological order. Assign responsibilities. Who will do What by When?
Establish completion dates for each step, working backwards, and allocate resources.

Ask what could go wrong & develop contingencies.

Evaluate progress and results, Express gratitude
Track progress, evaluate, make corrections, and continuously improve. Thank those involved.

3

Organizing Function

_____ ✕ _____

INTRODUCTION

The Organizing Function involves activities like establishing reporting relationships, determining the size and composition of your staff, creating position descriptions, defining job qualifications, etc. This chapter covers the following behavioral competencies:

Establishing Organization Structure – Task allocation, coordination, and supervision, which are directed towards the achievement of organizational aims. Types might include:

➤ Bureaucratic structure (role driven)
➤ Functional structure (position driven)
➤ Divisional structure (product driven)
➤ Matrix structure (project driven)

Defining Job Qualifications – Describing and recording aspects of jobs and specifying the skills and other requirements necessary to perform the job. This job analysis aims to answer questions such as:

1. Why does the job exist?
2. What physical and mental activities does the worker undertake?
3. When is the job to be performed?
4. Where is the job to be performed?
5. How does the worker do the job?
6. What qualifications are needed to perform the job?
7. What are the working conditions (such as levels of temperature, noise, offensive fumes, and light)?
8. What machinery or equipment is used in the job?
9. What constitutes successful performance?

Creating Position Descriptions – An explicit outline of essential functions, responsibilities and necessary requirements, and must include the following:

1. Job title, position number, and unit or department
2. Organizational relationship
3. Primary purpose of the position
4. General requirements; experience, education, special skills
5. Essential functions
6. Responsibilities and duties, in priority order

Applying GUIDE to the Organizing Competencies

Going from general to specific, the organization develops an over-all structure and draws an organizational chart to depict the division of labor to be used. Then, each department develops a division of labor indicating the specialization of work to be performed; so that, the department reaches its goals and contributes to over-all organizational success.

Establishing Organization Structure

Bureaucratic structures are role driven. Think military or government in which the needs, knowledge, and opinions of the workers (soldiers) are given less importance than strict obedience. In the words of Col. Nathan R. Jessup, "We follow orders or people die."

Functional structures are position driven. The vast majority of companies utilize a typical pyramid where the CEO and President are at the top followed by Vice Presidents, Managers, Supervisors, and Frontline Employees all categorized by function. Usually depicted like this:

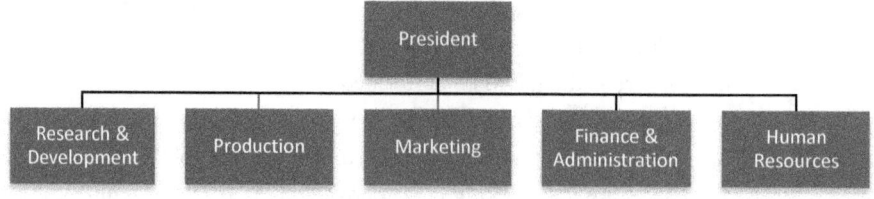

Divisional structures are product driven. Each division is responsible for only one product line and contains all the functional resources necessary to run the business. Literally, each division looks like a separate company. Depicted like this:

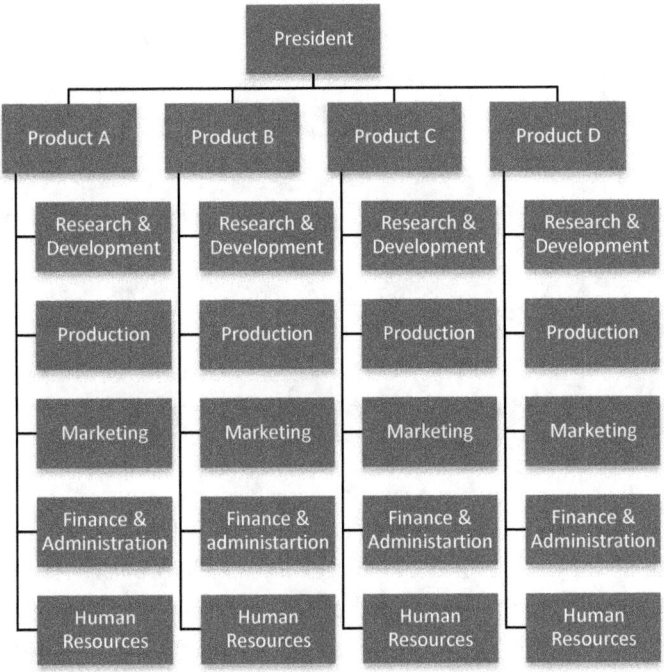

Matrix structures are project driven. When a project is sold, a Project Manager is assigned and he selects employees (using GUIDE of course) to fill the functional positions required from a pool of resources for that specialty. For example, a team of engineers would be required for the construction of an oil processing plant. The Project Manger would select a Chemical engineer from the Chemical engineers on staff, a Mechanical engineer from those on staff, etc. Consequently, each employee has two bosses; the functional boss, and the project boss. It looks like this:

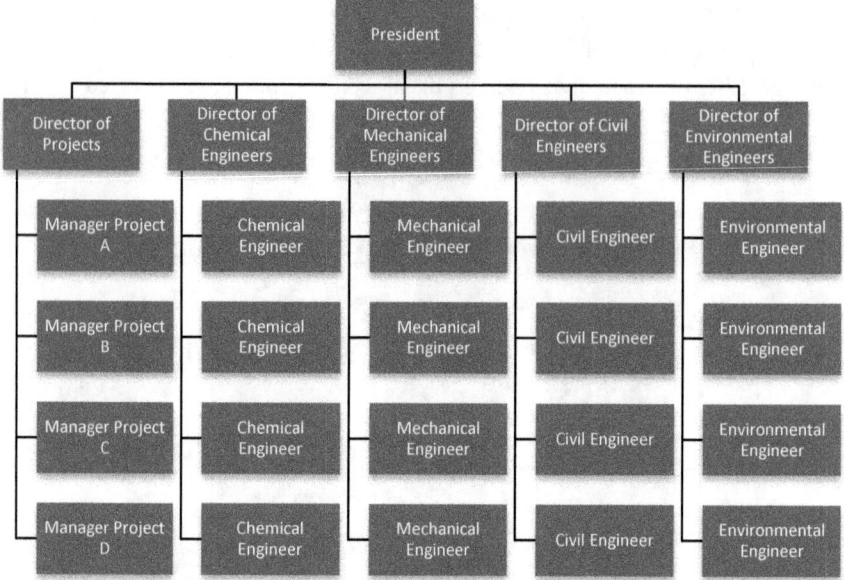

In most cases, the over-all organization structure has already been determined by upper management. You may be involved in decisions (See Chapter Four for use of GUIDE in Decision-Making) at a departmental level regarding the distribution of work or how many employees are required to carry out your mission.

Following the same rationale as the organization, departments can be organized by Function, Product or Service, or by Customer or Location.

Applying GUIDE to Defining Job Qualifications

The next step is to decide what work will be done by each position. Assume that your Human Resources Vice President has asked you to conduct a job analysis and create a position description for a self-directed team member. Here is how you could use GUIDE to facilitate that task.

Gather Information

Remember, gathering information means looking at what has happened historically. You'll need to interview people who know the job, such as a supervisor or incumbent in the current position. You might ask questions like:

> ➢ What are the daily responsibilities for this position?
> ➢ What kinds of situations and decisions impact this position?
> ➢ What are the biggest challenges in this position?
> ➢ What kind of training is required from the organization to get started?

> How important is technical knowledge for success in this position?
> What kinds of situations provide the most stress in this position?
> What is the nature of planning, meetings, presentations, analysis work, etc.?
> What would be the reason for someone doing poorly in the position?
> What provides the most satisfaction for successful incumbents?
> What do people like least about the job?

Understand the Available Information

This step is about verifying what's known. Seek the above information from other incumbents, supervisors, internal, and external customers to verify your assessment.

Investigate Alternatives

The future starts here. Conduct a meeting with three to seven decision-makers (five is optimal). Present a tentative list of essential functions and critical job qualifications. Essential functions are the physiological requirements of the job. This means what the person must lift, see, read, hear, etc. In my job, I must stand for long periods of time. Critical job qualifications are the behavioral competencies for the position (there are thirty managerial competencies listed in Chapter 1).

Ask the decision-makers for critical incidents in which an incumbent was either particularly effective or ineffective in performing the job responsibilities. Refine the list.

Decide on the Best Course of Action, Develop a Plan, and Do It

Ask the decision-makers to rank-order the competencies. Then prepare the final position description.

Evaluate Progress and Results, Express Gratitude

Send the position description to the powers that be and seek feedback. Revise as needed and use the document for your next hiring opportunity. Thank those involved for helping to complete the project.

It is likely that the Human Resources Department will conduct the job analysis or invite an external consultant to perform that task. Your role, most probably, will be to answer questions from the point of view of the incumbent or as supervisor of the incumbent. You might also be asked to participate in the Competency Determination meeting.

Creating Position Descriptions

Once the essential functions and competencies have been finalized, it's time to put together the Position Description.

On the following two pages is a position description based upon a Job Analysis. The following is a summary of the Job Analysis:

> ➤ The Team Member operates high speed paint mixing equipment, sets up all liquids and raw material, mixes ingredients, paying particular attention to temperatures and other settings.

> ➤ The Team Member then pumps paint from the dispersion equipment into the sand mill through the base pump and strains the product, following a flowchart procedure and batch ticket explicitly.

> ➤ The Team Member ensures that cans are ready for filling and that lids are on with the proper seal, places labels on cans and places the cans in boxes for shipping.

> ➤ The Team Member loads outgoing trucks with cases and pallets of finished product and unloads incoming trucks of raw materials and supplies.

> ➤ The Team Member ensures that all tanks are cleaned before another batch is run to avoid contamination of the formula or an out of specification color.

> ➤ The Team Member takes samples of product and tests the viscosity, weight, and tint strength, then enters the data into a computer and tests it again.

> ➤ The Team Member may need to adjust the batch, after testing the quality, to ensure the integrity of the product. This could be an adjustment in weight, viscosity, or color.

> ➤ The Team Member must work cooperatively with other team members, assisting in training, coaching, reinforcing, and providing support to teammates.

> ➤ The Team Member must work effectively in groups to accomplish organizational goals.

> ➤ The Team Member may have to modify plans or behavior in order to meet customer needs.

> ➤ The Team Member requires some computer literacy and may have to learn new technologies in a matter of hours.

> ➤ The Team Member needs to logically break down problems into essential elements, carryout diagnosis, and develop solutions.

Job Title: Team Member   Date: August 3, 2010

Job Number: TM50546   Unit TGC451

Reports To: Plant Director

Primary Purpose

The Team Member manufactures and packages paint products in accordance with quality standards and customer requirements.

General Requirements

- High school education
- Basic computer operation
- Aptitude for paint-mixing machine operation
- Previous experience in manufacturing setting (preferred)

Essential Functions

Standard abilities required:

- Lifts 40 to 50 pound bags of pigment, moves 55 gallon drums
- Reads and understands batch tickets several times a day
- Drives a lift truck
- Recognizes lot numbers and information on computer screens
- Differentiates sounds; such as, safety alarms, machine malfunctions, and completed batches
- Understands verbal instructions given at production meetings
- Speaks clearly when discussing production issues with other team members
- Physically removes blades from dispersion machines (takes two workers)
- Mentally stores information regarding production procedures, formula checks, etc.
- Ability to discern colors

Behavioral Competencies (in priority order)

1. Attention to Detail – Seeks completeness and accuracy in accomplishing tasks.
2. Safety Awareness – Is aware of conditions that affect employee safety and acts to prevent them.
3. Problem Analysis – Logically breaks down problems into their essential elements; carries out diagnosis, and develops solutions.
4. Teamwork – Works effectively with team, workgroup, or those outside formal authorities to accomplish organizational goals.
5. Communication – Expresses ideas effectively in individual and group situations; adjusts language or terminology to the characteristics and needs of the audience.
6. Ability to Learn – Quickly understands and applies information, concepts, and strategies.
7. Work Management – Plans work based upon availability of supplies and materials.
8. Adaptability – Ability to alter behavior and opinions in light of new information or changing situations.
9. Technical Knowledge – Has satisfactory level of technical skill or knowledge in position-related areas.
10. Motivational Fit – Personal satisfaction consistent with the job activities, organization values, and location of the work assigned.

This Position Description can be used to develop Selection Interview Guides (Chapter 9), Orient the New Employee (Chapter 10), Train on Job Skills (Chapter 11), Develop Organizational Talent (Chapter 12), and Manage Performance (Section Six). In short, the Behavioral Competencies are the core of the employee's business relationship and are used in everything from hiring to separation.

Undoubtedly, you have seen more traditional position descriptions that include sections on Nature and Scope of the Job, Responsibilities, Accountabilities, and Daily Duties. Rather than providing a generalized list for all employees, I believe these items should be covered specifically for each individual in Gaining Commitment to Performance Expectations (Chapter 22).

Organizing GUIDE

Gather information
Who, what, when, where, how, why regarding history of organizational structures, job qualifications and position descriptions in your area/department/team.

> **C**ommit
> **A**ffirm
> **R**ecognize
> **E**mpathize

Understand the available information
Check for understanding. Who would know?

Investigate alternatives
List all possible options based upon your organizing task.

Decide on the best course of action, Develop a plan, and Do it
Develop Organization Charts, Job Descriptions, Interview Guides, etc. Decide what actions come first, second, etc.

Evaluate progress and results, Express gratitude
Track progress, evaluate, make corrections, and continuously improve. Thank those involved.

4

Judgment

INTRODUCTION

Judgment is the most important dimension in life. People will be considered successful or not based upon the choices they make. There are three important aspects to judgment; Analyzing Problems, Making Decisions, and Decisiveness. This chapter covers these three behavioral competencies:

Analyzing Problems – Determining the cause of a deviation from expectations which includes the following components:

> Identifying deviations – Recognizing issues where there is a gap between what should be happening and what is actually happening.

> Collecting facts – Describing and recording aspects of the problem and specifying:

  1. What is the problem?
  2. Where does it exist?
  3. When did you first notice it?
  4. What is the scope?

> Interpreting data – Examining the data to find uniqueness. Answering:

  1. What's unique?
  2. What's been altered?

> Developing conclusions – Formulating a preliminary cause statement.

> Creating hypothesis – A statement of the most probable cause.

> Verifying cause – Examining, investigating, or soliciting proof of the hypothesis.

Making Decisions – Choosing between various alternatives for correcting the deviation.

➤ Choosing a method – Based upon the objectives of the decision, choosing a decision model to be used.

➤ Generating alternatives – Using the specified model, create a list of all options.

➤ Selecting a solution – Evaluating the alternatives against the decision criteria, choose the one that best meets the criteria. Anticipate potential problems and establish contingencies based upon seriousness and probability.

Decisiveness – Implementing the decision with little or no hesitation.

Applying GUIDE to Analyzing Problems, Making Decisions, and Decisiveness

Given the three dimensions of judgment, GUIDE is divided among them. Analyzing the problem entails completing the G & U steps of GUIDE. Assuming the problem as stated is worth correcting, making the decision requires completing the I & D steps of GUIDE. Decisiveness involves the D & E steps of GUIDE.

Gather Information

This step is analogous to a doctor exploring symptoms to diagnose a patient's illness. You might ask questions like:

1. What is the problem? Define the deviation from what should be happening and the thing, process, or person with the gap.
2. Where does it exist? Where on the thing, process, or person and where in the country, city, or local site?
3. When did you first notice it? In clock or calendar time and if this is a process, when in the steps of the process was it noticed?
4. What is the scope? Scope may mean how many units in a run, how many parts of the unit, and what is the trend (better or worse)?

It would be useful to think of what could be going wrong and compare those things to what is actually going wrong. This will help complete the next step.

Understand the Available Information

This step is about examining the data to find uniqueness between what is happening and what might be happening instead. It is important to frame how you think about its causes. Because, how you analyze an issue - what questions you ask about it - determines the types of solutions that you will consider. The two most important questions to verify are:

1. What's unique? In other words, what is different about the facts of this issue compared to a similar thing, process, or person?
2. What's been altered? Given the distinctions from the previous question, what has changed in any of them around the time you first noticed the discrepancy?

Before moving to the next step in GUIDE, three things are essential:

- ➢ Formulate a conclusion – a preliminary cause statement.
- ➢ Create your hypothesis – A statement of the most probable cause. This cause must explain all the observed facts.
- ➢ Verify the cause by examining, investigating, or soliciting proof of the hypothesis.

Finally, decide whether this problem is worth correcting. The effect of the problem may be very costly and require a fix. In some cases, the effect of the problem is not significant and may be ignored. Therefore, the first decision is a "Go" or "No-Go" choice.

*I*nvestigate Alternatives

Moving into this step assumes that a "Go" decision has been made. Now is the time to look toward the future. While the future is uncertain, the purpose of this step is to explore the alternatives and measure them against some relatively objective criterion.

What is the purpose of the decision? Is it to think of solutions to a malfunction in a manufacturing process? Is it to determine what to do to move toward a goal which has not been achieved? Is it to create a new product or to re-engineer an old product that has been losing market share? Is it to determine how to reach six-sigma process quality? Is it to choose the best supplier of your raw materials?

Whatever the purpose, the first part of this step is to choose a model, based upon the objectives of the decision. This could be a very conventional method; such as, brainstorming or force field analysis, or it could be a very creative method like movie magic. In any case, this step is about employing developmental thinking. That means absolutely no criticism of any alternatives.

The second phase is to set the criteria. List the "must haves," those criteria that represent knock out conditions. The fewer the better, three to five are recommended. For example, let's say you plan to buy a house. The three most important criteria might be price, location, and size. You might write these on your list:

1. Price < $250,000
2. Location = best school district
3. Size > 2500 square feet

Notice the three quality values. For price, the value is less than or smaller is better. For location, the value is equal to or optimal is best. For size, the value is greater than or larger is better. This means, if the price is $250,000.01 the house will be eliminated from the list of alternatives and not be considered further. If the house is one foot outside the school district of choice, it will not be considered further. If the size is 2499 square feet, it's out. Any one of these criteria can knock the alternative out of consideration.

Next, consider the desirable criteria. List the "wants," those criteria that represent the most desirable conditions. These things might include:

1. A swimming pool
2. Landscaping
3. A modern kitchen
4. Three-car garage
5. Five bedrooms
6. A media room

While everyone has unlimited wants, it would be advisable to limit the number of wants to about ten or fewer. Also, notice that five bedrooms is another way to measure size, which means that you may wish to use a criterion in both lists. The square footage in the "must" list is used as a knockout and the five bedrooms can be used to contrast how well each alternative meets the stated need. In other words, the more bedrooms a house has the higher its score.

The way scoring works is two-fold. First, assign a weight to the wants. The weight represents the relative importance of the criteria. Use a ten point scale like so:

1. A swimming pool   10
2. Landscaping   5
3. A modern kitchen   7
4. Three-car garage   7
5. Five bedrooms   8
6. A media room   9

If you prefer, you may rearrange the criteria so they are in descending order showing which have the highest priority to the decision. Notice that a numeric value may be used for more than one criterion.

The second aspect to scoring involves how well an alternative satisfies your desire. One method is to use a multiplier; such as, high (3 points), medium (2 points), low (1 point), and none (0 points). For instance, let's say you look at four houses. The first house has a wonderful pool with landscaping, rock formations, four waterfalls, and a fireplace in the spa (*Oooh!*). You feel highly satisfied; so, you multiply the weight by the multiplier and give this alternative 30 points (10 x 3). The second house has a very plain pool but didn't pass the "must haves" criteria. The third house has no pool and therefore gets zero points (10 x 0). The fourth house moderately satisfies your pool desire and gets 20 points (10 x 2).

The third phase is to compare alternatives. In our example of purchasing a house, this phase is easier with the help of a real estate agent. Provide the agent with your must criteria, take a road trip to collect data on each available house, and take notes to be used in the evaluation later. Finally, put together a matrix like this one:

MUST HAVES		Alt. #1	Alt. #2	Alt. #3	Alt. #4
Price < $250,000		$218,900	$110,400	$195,900	$215,600
Location = best school district		√	√	√	√
Size > 2500 SF		3030	1600	2600	2875
WANTS	**Weights**	Multipliers – H=3, M=2, L=1, N=0			
Swimming pool	10	30		0	20
Media room	9	27		27	18
Five bedrooms	8	16		8	24
Modern kitchen	7	7		21	14
Three-car garage	7	14		21	14
Landscaping	5	10		15	5
	Total	104		92	95

Decide on the Best Course of Action, Develop a Plan, and Do It

Choose a course of action based upon the best information and relative impact among alternatives as compared to the decision criteria chosen. In this case, place an offer on the house with the highest points. Decisiveness comes into play here. Don't hesitate.

Evaluate Progress and Results, Express Gratitude

A part of this evaluation can be made before the final decision is made. In the previous step, Alternative #1 was chosen based upon its highest point total. Let's look at the choice compared to some other considerations. Ask some "what if..." questions, like:

> ➢ "What could go wrong with Alternative #1?"
> ➢ "What if they don't accept the offer?"
> ➢ "Could we put a pool in Alternative #3 for the price difference?"
> ➢ "What if we cannot move into the house in a timely manner?"

Ultimately, the evaluation of this decision can only happen after you have moved into the house. It may take months or even years before you can be certain that the choice was the right one. This post mortem evaluation will help in similar or future decisions.

Use the Problem Solving GUIDE on the next page the next time you have a situation requiring problem analysis or decision making.

ProblemSolving GUIDE

Gather information
What's the problem? Where does it exist? When did you first notice it?
What is the scope?

> **C**ommit
> **A**ffirm
> **R**ecognize
> **E**mpathize

Understand the available information
Check for understanding (yours and theirs). What's unique? What's been altered? Is your hypothesis
logical?

Investigate alternatives
State the purpose. Determine decision criteria. Determine relative importance of desirables. List the
alternatives. Determine which alternative best meets the need.

Decide on the best course of action, Develop a plan, and Do it
Choose the best alternative as compared to the decision criteria. Don't hesitate.

Evaluate progress and results, Express gratitude
Evaluate what could go wrong and consider contingencies.

Section Two

Fundamental Skills
of Communicating

5

General Communication Concepts

INTRODUCTION

A colleague of mine used to say, "Communication is the second most abused word in the English language." Although a punch line followed the statement, look up the word communicate in the dictionary and you'll find, "transmit disease" and "give or receive Communion" among the varied definitions. Entire books have been devoted to communication. As I write this, Amazon.com lists 295,990 books with "Communication" in the title.

Undeniably, communication takes on many faces. The vast majority of my career has been spent teaching people to communicate better. In fact, over two-thirds of this book is devoted to communicating face-to-face with one or more other people. This chapter covers these four behavioral competencies:

Selecting a Method – determining the best channel to use based upon the purpose and importance of the message. Types might include:

- ➢ Formal presentation
- ➢ Written (letter, memo, e-mail, etc.)
- ➢ One-to-one
- ➢ Media

Imparting a Message – verbal, vocal, and visual interchange of thoughts, opinions, or information to the intended recipient.

Receiving Feedback – decoding the message and giving the sender a reaction to it.

Making Corrections – confirming the feedback and resending the message for clarification

What is Communication?

The dictionary defines communication this way:

the imparting or interchange of thoughts, opinions, or information by speech, writing, or sign

The Wikipedia definition may seem too academic:

Communication is a process whereby information is enclosed in a package and is channeled and imparted by a sender to a receiver via some medium. The receiver then decodes the message and gives the sender a feedback.

However, it can be interpreted like this:

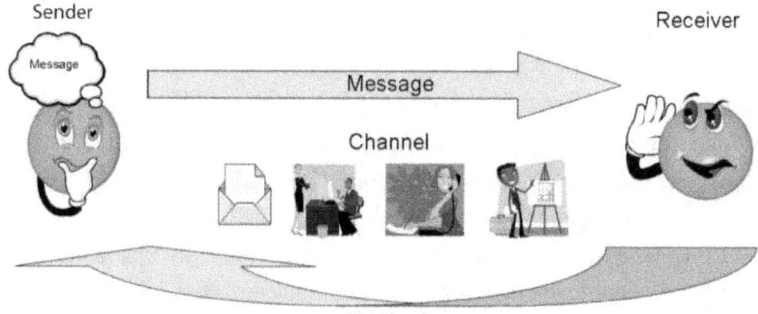

Why Do People Communicate?

➤ To Socialize
➤ To Negotiate
➤ To Educate
➤ To Entertain
➤ To Network
➤ To Lead

Ultimately, the purpose for all communication is to *persuade*! To buy, fund, invest, use, choose, change, approve, accept, adopt, award, etc.

How Do People Communicate?

➤ Auditory – Speech, Song
➤ Non-Verbal – Body Language, Tone of Voice, Sign Language (gestures), Paralanguage (pitch, volume, intonation), Touch, Eye Contact
➤ Media – Pictures, Graphics, Writing, Sound

Barriers to Communication

Barriers to communication come in a wide variety of shapes and sizes. The term scholars use for factors that block effective communication is "noise." Here are some examples:

> **Conditional Noise**: Tangibles that can make concentration difficult; including, room temperature, road or building repairs, overly bright or dim lighting, air pollution, wall color, annoying people, etc.

> **Cultural Noise**: Assumptions in regard to religion, gender, ethnics, national origin, or generational differences can cause misunderstandings. Often these faux pas are the result of ignorance. For example, a person might say, "Have a happy Yom Kippur" to a Jew. Knowing it's a religious holiday and assuming it to be a celebration. However, Yom Kippur is not a day of celebration. It is the day Jews seek forgiveness for any wrong they have done against God or to humans. Misinterpretations in any of these realms could lead one or both parties to consider the other insensitive, illiterate, shiftless, unsympathetic, etc.

> **Emotional Noise**: Focus can be affected by one's disposition. This may involve extreme agitation caused by outside sources or other psychological disorders.

> **Lexical Noise**: Grammatical shifts in number, tense, subject, voice, or point of view can cause irritation. People are increasingly using "their" as a singular pronoun. For example, "A person who uses 'their' as a singular pronoun needs 'their' head examined." Another error gaining momentum is the use of "him and I." A man referring to a prize his son and he had won stated it was "...exciting for him and I." The correct phrase is "...for him and me."

> **Lingual Noise**: Vocabulary choice can interfere with the meaning of the message. If I say, "Men are more 'sensitive' about status than women," sensitive can be interpreted in several ways. Do you think it means men get "physical sensations," are "excessively affected," have "acute mental awareness," or are "easily annoyed" by status? By the way, is that a good thing or a bad thing?

- ➢ **Physical-Disorder Noise**: Any damage or disease that prevents the listener from interpreting the message accurately; such as, hearing or vision problems.
- ➢ **Structural Noise**: Disorderly composition lacks clarity. A speaker says he is going to make three points, but then lists five. This causes undue confusion.

Suffice it to say that many things can go wrong when two or more people try to communicate. For that reason, communication must be a dynamic process. The effective communicator seeks to understand the other person's point of view and meaning.

Communication 101

Used together, these three things will impact your probability of success:

- ➢ Verbal – the words used to speak, write, and sing; includes vocabulary, sentence structure, and grammar.
- ➢ Vocal – the sounds used; includes tone of voice, word emphasis, articulation, tempo, pitch, and volume.
- ➢ Visual – what the receiver sees; includes body language, gestures, eye contact, facial expression, actions, and audiovisual aids.

Persuasive Communication

Persuasiveness requires credibility with your audience. There are many ways to build credibility. Some of these include being perceived as competent, confident and caring. In order to convince someone to buy your ideas, evidence is essential. There are two kinds of evidence:

1. Concrete = factual, objective, quantitative
2. Conceptual = feelings, subjective, qualitative

People will respond to how they feel first and then seek facts to support or confirm those feelings. People shape their perceptions and reach conclusions as a result of a dynamic interplay between logic and emotions.

With that in mind you'll want to present statistics and research results that have an emotional tie to the people you are trying to influence. Some examples of useful quantitative data are: census data, market research, product test results, and scientific measurements.

Interspersing personal examples or verbal illustrations will also increase your probability of success. You might use; personal experiences, experiences of others, hypothetical situations, or human interest stories to enhance the statistical evidence.

Another influential tactic is the use of contrasts and comparisons. A contrast highlights the distinct difference between two things; while comparisons identify similarities between or among things. You contrast a Jaguar with a Ford Focus; while you compare a Jaguar to a BMW and a Mercedes Benz.

Applying GUIDE to Influencing

*G*ather Information

Frequently, people try to influence others by offering information in the form of evidence that represents their advocacy. Subconsciously, they may feel a need to show that their idea is the right one or the best one. Surprisingly, this tactic decreases the probability of success because it makes others feel like they must defend their position.

Seeking information from others regarding their feelings about the issue has been proven to be a more influential tactic. Suppose the Director of Administration has instituted a policy that you would like to change. You might ask the Director questions like:

> ➤ "Why did you institute this policy?"
> ➤ "What was the objective of this decision?"
> ➤ "Who was involved in the decision?"
> ➤ "What other possibilities did you consider?"
> ➤ "When did you start this practice?"
> ➤ "Where have you seen improvement?"
> ➤ "Have you noticed any adverse consequences from the decision?"
> ➤ "What effect does this have on workforce morale?"

Suffice it to say the purpose of these questions is to help the Director discover the negative implications to the decision without you stating them explicitly. Each subsequent question is dependent upon the answer to the previous question, which requires quick thinking. Your goal is to get the other person to figure out that the current situation is negative. If you can help the Director figure it out, then influencing a change becomes significantly easier.

Depending upon the context of the issue under discussion, the implications might include; turnover, decreased quality, loss of productivity, customer dissatisfaction, loss of revenue, increased operating cost, etc.

*U*nderstand the Available Information

This step is about verifying what you know. You might summarize what you've heard in the previous step like this:

"So, Director, your objective for this new policy was to reduce expenses. It seems to have worked somewhat, but you would be open to other alternatives as long as costs are reduced. Is that right?"

*I*nvestigate Alternatives

The future starts here. At this stage you might want to seek alternatives to the solution that was originally selected. However, be prepared to offer several ideas that might replace the one chosen. A good starting place is to begin with three that you think will work. Explain each idea completely and offer the reason why you think it would have a better outcome than the one currently in place. For instance:

> ➤ "Would you be interested in a way to control cost on _____?"
> ➤ "If we could come up with a way to reduce cost in other areas would you be willing to revive the previous policy on _____?"
> ➤ "Can you think of any other areas where cost may be too high?"
> ➤ "Now that you mention it, what if we were able to reduce inventory levels...?"

These types of questions focus the other party on solution alternatives. If done well, the Director will be telling you the benefits of implementing alternate solutions.

*D*ecide on the Best Course of Action, *D*evelop a Plan, and *D*o It

Select the alternative that best matches the goal of your influence. Then ask:

"Who needs to do what and by when to implement the solution?"

There may be other questions you'll want to ask to pin down the plan of action; but who, what, and when are the most important.

*E*valuate Progress and Results, *E*xpress Gratitude

Finally, express gratitude to the Director for helping to make the situation better. You might say something like:

"I really appreciate you giving me the time to discuss this important matter. I think the plan we worked out here will pay-off and benefit the workforce considerably. Thank you."

Full evaluation of the progress and results will have to wait until the plan is implemented and may take weeks or even months before results can be documented.

Are You Listening?

Effective communication requires a speaker (sender) and at least one listener (receiver), as shown in the Communication Model. The only way the speaker knows if the listener heard the message correctly is when the listener becomes the speaker and provides feedback to the original sender.

God gave us two ears and one mouth. His intent was for us to use them proportionally. Especially if the purpose of your communication is to persuade, as mentioned in the previous section, the most influential behavior is to seek from others. It then holds that you should pay attention to the answers to your questions.

Let's explore four ways you might demonstrate that you received the message. They include:

> ➤ Gathering Information
> ➤ Paraphrasing
> ➤ Responding with Empathy
> ➤ Providing SPIN Feedback

Gathering Information

Effective questions can be useful at any time. Even in the formal GUIDE process, one could retreat to the Gather stage if more information is needed. There are three types of questions:

> ➤ Questions for information
> ➤ Questions masking an opinion
> ➤ Questions masking disagreement

Questions for information represent a sincere, genuine request using who, what, when, where, why, and sometimes how form. Once you have heard the message you might respond with:

> "Who are we talking about?" "What do you think the cause of that is?" "When do you want to start the project?" "Where in the process did you first notice the problem?" "Why do you think the pump stopped?" "How can we best resolve the issue?"

Sometimes people ask questions that are really masks for either an opposing opinion or for disagreement. For example, if someone said, "Couldn't we have purchased a software package and avoided this problem?" What's behind the question is most likely an opinion. The person believes if different software had been in place there would have been no problem. Asking a question like that rather than just stating the opinion can cause animosity between the two parties. It can come across as sarcastic or condescending; so, it would be advisable to just state the opinion.

Similarly, the listener might mask a disagreement like this, "Do you *really* think that's the best way to handle this situation?" Clearly, the subtext is disagreement. It would be better to simply say that you have some concerns and state them.

Paraphrasing

An effective way to show that you understand the message is paraphrasing. There are two types of paraphrasing:

> Paraphrasing content
> Paraphrasing intent

Paraphrasing content means summarizing the message in your own words. It's a rephrased, simplified, and usually shorter version of what was said.

For instance, one of your employees says, "Personnel hasn't sent me the forms to be mailed, so the requests will be late this month."

Paraphrasing the content might sound like this, "Let me make sure I understand what you're saying. Tom's people haven't printed the employee documents for our monthly performance appraisal mailing. Is that right?"

It is very important to paraphrase to the satisfaction of the speaker. In other words, before you refute what someone says, you need to make sure you understand it completely. Often people listen just enough to formulate a rebuttal, then offer a counter argument which may alienate the other person. Listening to rebut instead of to understand can lead to disagreements, mistrust, or other long-term consequences. Therefore, it's important to paraphrase and then ask, "Is that right?" If you got it, the speaker will say, "Yes, that's right," and you can move on. If you did not get it, the speaker has an opportunity to clarify the message.

Paraphrasing for intent means determining what the other person's purpose is. For example, what if your boss said, "Effective immediately, everyone will send correspondence to me for editing."

This could be seen as a way to ensure the department produces exceptional work or it could be perceived as punishment or distrust. To paraphrase for intent one might say, "Is that to keep customers happy or have we been making mistakes?"

Responding with Empathy

While listening, pay particular attention to how the message is expressed. You may notice words used or body language that expresses feelings. When responding to these signals, reply with empathy. Showing empathy helps reduce tension and lower resistance. Be specific and sincere by including these two components:

> Recap the content of the speaker's message
> State the feelings expressed in the message

For example, you might say, "Not being allowed to speak at the conference, after you prepared so hard must be very disappointing." See Appendix A for tips on what you can say to show empathy.

Providing SPIN Feedback

In some cases providing SPIN feedback, which was discussed in Chapter 1, might be the more appropriate tactic to show you are listening. Remember to include all of the following four elements:

> Situation
> Performance
> Impact
> Next time

Here's an example of positive feedback using SPIN:

S – "When you were talking to that customer,"

P – "You said, 'I wish I could fix it. I know it's annoying to be waiting such a long time. Unfortunately, this will require an expert from our Service Department. I'll call one for you and set up an appointment. It shouldn't take that long.'"

I – "The customer was put at ease because you were empathetic."

N – "You will continue to have success if you handle similar situations the same way in the future."

Here's an example of corrective feedback using SPIN:

S – "That woman was upset because her product hasn't worked properly since it was installed."

P – "You told her, 'The service contract should have been explained to you by the installer...' and that she'd 'just have to wait.'"

I – "She said, 'I guess I don't have much choice do I?' and walked off in a huff."

N – "Next time, you might try apologizing and checking with her to find out what she needs. Say something like, 'I'm sorry the service contract wasn't explained to you Mrs. Riley. Are you concerned that the delay will cost you more money?' Then assuming that is her concern, you could assure her that there would be no additional charges. Let her know that you will take personal responsibility to get the Service Technician to her as soon as possible. By handling it that way, you'd reduce her anxiety and help solve her problem.

Use the Influencing GUIDE on the following page to plan important discussions.

Influencing GUIDE

Gather information
Seek audience input 1st Offer your input 2nd Tell story, shocking example, dramatic statistic

> Commit
> Affirm
> Recognize
> Empathize

Understand the available information
Summarize why the problem exist, is significant   Check for agreement

Investigate alternatives
Seek ideas to solve the issue or provide specific, viable solutions

Decide on the best course of action, Develop a plan, and Do it
Tell the audience what will happen if the solution is implemented versus not; then, call for action

Evaluate progress and results, Express gratitude
Thank audience for meeting.   Express confidence in carrying out the solution

6

Formal Presentations

INTRODUCTION

The previous chapter contains a set of barriers to communication referred to as noise, all of which apply to public speaking as well. Speaking before groups of three to one thousand may create stress due to the dynamics caused by the size of the audience.

Additional Barriers

- ➢ Fear of public speaking
- ➢ Procrastination
- ➢ Poor structure
- ➢ Not engaging the audience
- ➢ Ignoring room arrangements

Fear of Public Speaking

Since the first Book of Lists was published in 1977, fear of public speaking has been ranked either number one or number two on the list. Fear of Death ranks seventh, meaning people would rather die than stand before a group and try to articulate their thoughts. Anxiety can be debilitating. Sammy Davis, Jr. once said, "Everybody gets butterflies. The trick is to get them to fly in formation."

Procrastination

If you have a tendency to procrastinate, it can add to the anxiety. Indeed, planning and ample preparation tends to reduce the fear. My confidence goes up the more I rehearse and the times when I've been the most nervous have been when I didn't feel I knew the material well enough. Joel Weldon, the best professional speaker I've ever seen, suggests a 10-1 ratio. That is preparing 10 hours for every 1 hour presentation.

Poor Structure

Poor structure makes it more difficult for the audience to follow the message. I was in the audience at a presentation where the speaker said, "Tonight I have three main points..." When he got to main point number five, I was lost. Listeners won't respond affirmatively if the presentation is disorganized, which causes you more anxiety.

Not Engaging the Audience

One of the most important things a speaker can do is relate to the audience. In most situations, formal presentations should not be strictly lectures. Involve the audience by asking questions like, "What does this mean to you?" or, "How can you apply this in your job?" Always try to get the audience to think about using the material, not just sit and listen.

Ignoring Room Arrangements

Factors that can make or break your presentation include: room set-up, seating arrangement, lighting, air conditioning or heating control, handouts, audio visual equipment, etc.

DEVELOPING YOUR PRESENTATION OR SPEECH

Let's apply the fundamental functions of managing to public speaking. They are:

1. Planning
2. Organizing
3. Leading
4. Controlling

Planning

Planning requires you to answer a variety of questions in analyzing the situation. For instance, you will want to know:

➤ What is my subject?
➤ Why is my subject important to this audience?
➤ How many people will be attending?
➤ What is the desired outcome?
➤ How much time will I have?
➤ What do I need to know about the audience?

1. Is it predominantly one age group
2. Education of the majority
3. Gender mix

    4.   Geographic location

    5.   Occupation

    6.   Social or economic status

    7.   Special interests

> When can I get into the room to rehearse or set-up before the presentation?

> What other information do I need from my key contact?

Organizing

Here are three options for organizing your presentation. You can use them individually or together.

Mind Mapping

One way to organize your thoughts is to develop a tree-like diagram. The term "mind map" was coined and trade marked by Tony Buzan, a BBC personality.

Buzan suggests the following guidelines for creating mind maps:

1. Start in the center with an image of the topic, using at least 3 colors.
2. Use images, symbols, codes, and dimensions throughout your mind map.
3. Select key words and print using upper or lower case letters.
4. Each word/image is best alone and sitting on its own line.
5. The lines should be connected, starting from the central image. The central lines are thicker, organic and thinner as they radiate out from the center.
6. Make the lines the same length as the word/image they support.
7. Use multiple colors throughout the mind map, for visual stimulation and also to encode or group.
8. Develop your own personal style of mind mapping.
9. Use emphasis and show associations in your mind map.
10. Keep the mind map clear by using radial hierarchy, numerical order or outlines to embrace your branches.

Outlining

Here is an example of an outline format using GUIDE:

    I.   Gather information (Give information)

        A. Capture attention

        B. Build interest or anticipation

II. Understand the available information (Summary of need)

III. Investigate alternatives (Seek or provide ideas and add)
   A. W. I. I. F. M.
      1. Advantages
      2. Improvements

   B. Substantiating material (Choose one to three)
      1. Describe your personal experience
      2. Draw a persuasive analogy
      3. Quote a recognized expert
      4. Explain an instance of success or precedent
      5. Provide substantiating statistics
      6. Supply your research results

IV. Decide on the best course of action, Develop a plan, and Do it (Your conclusion)

V. Evaluate progress and results, Express gratitude (Call to action)

Storyboarding

Technically, storyboards are a set of sketches arranged in sequence on panels, outlining the scenes that will make up something to be filmed, such as, a motion picture, television show, or advertisement. You may find storyboards useful in preparing for a speech as well.

Speech Component - (Opening)

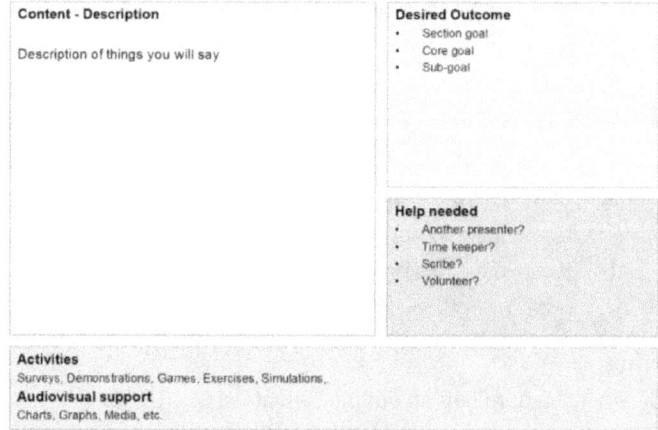

Now it's time to write the speech. The actual presentation will follow the GUIDE format, however, when you write the components, you need to create them in a different order.

Write the **I** first because it is the essence of your speech. Once that is completed then it's easier to go to the **U** and write a preview of what you're going to tell them. Then go to the **D** to explain what you just told them. Next, write the **G** as a dramatic opening. Finally, write the **E** as a compelling call to action.

Components of the Presentation (assume a 30 minute speech)

Gather information (1 minute)

Capturing the audience attention is paramount. If you start with, "Good evening my name is Joe Speaks…." the first impression may be that you are more interested in yourself than in the audience. To build interest or anticipation, start with one of the following:

> - An interesting or amusing anecdote
> - A quote that supports the theme of the presentation
> - An assertion of your hypothesis as if it were a fact
> - A definition of the most significant concept in your speech
> - A rhetorical question regarding the main point
> - A scenario or projected sequence of events
> - A clip of inspirational music, slide show, or movie

Understand the available information (1 minute)

Tell them what you're going to tell them by summarizing the need or main points of the speech. This helps the audience anticipate the main message and is a good bridge to the core section of the presentation.

Investigate alternatives – (3 key points - 7 minutes/point)

This is the core section of the speech. This is where you will seek or provide ideas for handling the situation whether it is a problem to be solved, a plan to be implemented, or a decision to be made. The most effective presentations limit the number of ideas here to three. While in the organizing stage, you may have many more than three ideas. You'll need to reduce the list to the three most important, useful, or likely to be implemented ideas.

The first step in reducing the list is to decide what model would make the most sense based upon your subject and audience?

> - Compare or contrast
> - General to specific
> - Order of Importance

> ➤ Regional organization
> ➤ Sequential progression
> ➤ Subjective approach
> ➤ Specific to general

Allow five minutes at the end of this section for questions. It is important to do it now so you maintain control of the presentation. Many speakers wait to ask for questions until they have closed and then the end fizzles. You want to regain control of the group, review the message, and close with drama.

Decide on the best course of action – (30 seconds)

Tell them what you've told them by restating the key points, but avoid redundancy. Use synonyms when you summarize the main ideas. Reinforce the message through comparisons or contrasts. Prepare a smooth transition to the Grand Finale.

Evaluate – (30 seconds)

The Call to Action may be different depending upon the purpose of the speech. Ask yourself, "What is the take away for the audience?" One option may be to provide a reminder from the core message. If the purpose is training, suggest how to apply the skills learned during the next month. This is your final opportunity to close the sale, ask for the order, request approval, etc.

Leading

Don's Top Ten Things to Add Impact, Interest, and Variety

1. **Stories** – are the best way to increase audience retention by sharing ideas and concepts in a way that PowerPoint slides can't. Good stories amaze the audience and make people think or feel differently about a subject. They can show the audience how to apply what is to be learned and used.

    In order to be good, stories must contain compelling characters, be clear and concise, use evocative and emotive language, and be spoken naturally.

2. **Humor** – sparks interest and involves the audience in the presentation. If they're not laughing they're not listening. Humor is not telling jokes. Rather it involves using a humorous speech pattern. Think of how Bill Cosby tells stories. He doesn't say funny things. He says things funny.

    I like to build on something that happens naturally in the room. I don't make fun of someone else, but I will make fun of myself.

3.   **Effective Audiovisuals** – clarify and support the message. The best visual aids are the real thing. If you're going to teach me how to use a pressure cooker, bring the pressure cooker. The next best visuals will be photographs, drawings, or cartoons that support the spoken word without more words. Third best would include charts, graphs, or pictographs that represent statistical data in a colorful entertaining way.

Consider using movies, music, or voice recordings as a way to introduce a topic. A friend of mine once opened a presentation on upward mobility in the organization by playing Billy Joel's "Movin' Out." These methods access all the learning styles and create a memorable experience.

4.   **Never Let 'Em See You Sweat** – even though you're nervous The key is to remember no one in the audience knows your intentions, so don't apologize if you stumble. Rather, pretend that was what you intended to do. Proper posture projects confidence. If you're hands are shaking, place your notes on a podium.

Above all, rehearse. The better you know the material, the less nervous you'll be.

5.   **Be Assertive** – means speak with conviction. Declare your ideas as if they are true. By being assertive, you are perceived as decisive, self-assured, confident, and encouraging.

Passive speakers on the other hand, are perceived as tentative, uncertain, and submissive. Aggressive speakers are perceived as militant, overly competitive, and threatening.

6.   **Modulate Vocal Qualities** – means pay attention to pitch, volume, rate, and tone.

   ➤ Pitch relates to how high or low the frequency of the sound, from shrill to deep. The higher the pitch, the more nervous you appear and the harder it is on your vocal cords. Try to lower your pitch an octave to reduce the stress on your larynx. You'll sound more confident and be able to speak longer.

   ➤ Volume relates to the loudness of the sound, from yelling to whispering. While whispering may be a way to get someone's attention, it is rare that yelling will have a positive effect. I like to pretend that my voice is a physical object, like a ball, and I need to bounce it off the back wall. Your volume needs to be loud enough for people in the back of the room to hear without blasting the front row.

➤ Rate relates to the speed of the speech, from < 100 to > 250 words per minute (wpm). Shoot for between 140 – 170 wpm. You'll want to change the rate periodically. Joel Weldon says he speaks at 250 wpm with gusts to 500. A person can hear and comprehend a speaker whose rate is 500 wpm, but wouldn't want that to continue for more than 30 minutes unbroken. Similarly, the audience can take less than 100 wpm for a short time, but would fall asleep if it went on very long.

➤ Tone relates to the emotional impact of the voice, from angry to calm. You'll want to consider changing the tone based upon the subject or the effect you desire at a particular section of the speech. If the anecdote is from a child's perspective, give your voice a childish tone. If the purpose of the declaration is serious, use a grave tone. If the question is rhetorical, perhaps a bit of sarcasm might be appropriate.

7. **Be Aware of Speech Patterns** – which are habits that can interfere with the listener's train of thought. Examples include: up speak, mumbling, mispronunciation, fillers like "a" and "um."

8. **Exercise Your Diaphragm!** – by breathing properly. Vocal power is associated with awareness, ability, and certainty.

9. **Practice Visual Cues** – such as facial expressions, eye contact, gestures, and hand and body movements.

➤ Facial expressions must match the emotion in the words. If the message is happy, smile. If the message is sad, frown.

➤ The more eye contact you have with audience members the better. I try to maintain eye contact with each person for 3 to 5 seconds before moving to another person.

➤ Gestures need to match the message as well. If I'm using the word "huge," my arms will be spread as wide as I can make them. If I'm using the word "tiny," my thumb and index fingers will be nearly touching.

➤ Hand and body movements need a purpose as well. Don't pace like a caged animal. Move your body and your hands to animate the story as an actor would on stage.

10. **Pace the Presentation** – efficiently to keep the audience alert. Move to different points on the stage. Change the form of delivery from lecture, to audio visual, to activity, to application exercise. Individual stories or anecdotes should be no longer than 2-3 minutes each.

Three Types of Questions and How to Handle Them

These three types of questions were presented in the previous chapter from the perspective of listening. Now let's consider what happens when you are presenting and an audience member asks you questions. What do you do when the questions are coming at you? The three types of questions are:

1. Questions for information
2. Questions masking an opinion
3. Questions masking disagreement

Questions for information are sincere, genuine requests. They usually start with Who, What, When, Where, Why, and How. Such as; "Who is responsible for making changes to this policy?" "What exactly do you expect us to do after this meeting is over?" "When is the deadline for submitting a new proposal?" "Where can we find the data necessary to prepare the financial plan?" "Why is this important for us?" "How can we learn the new system?"

The way to prepare for these types of questions is to:

1. Expect questions. As you are planning your speech consider what questions you would ask. Think about your audience and determine who among them may ask questions and what those questions might be.

2. Prepare answers for the most likely questions. If there is more than one, pick the best among them.

3. Review the content of the speech and add material to cover the most significant questions.

4. Rehearse your presentation in front of a few people and have them ask questions so you feel comfortable hearing the questions come from the floor.

Questions masking an opinion start with phrases like, "Don't you think…", "Wouldn't it be better to…", "Isn't it okay to…" For instance, "Don't you think what matters most is to stay within budget?" "Wouldn't it be better to let the customer decide how to handle the delivery?" "Isn't it okay to negotiate different terms with each customer?"

The way to handle these types of questions is to:

1. Hear the person out. You may want to take notes if the question gets lengthy.
2. Paraphrase your understanding of the idea until the originator agrees that you fully understand it.
3. Use the most appropriate CARE behavior. If you think the person's idea is worthy of consideration, Affirm the person. If not, perhaps Empathy would be more appropriate.
4. Answer the question.

Questions masking disagreement are usually a bit more hostile sounding. For instance, "You don't seriously expect us to act that way do you?" "Do *you* agree with that approach?" "Can *you* calculate the cost of quality?"

The way to handle these types of questions is to:

1. Make sure you understand the disagreement. You might say, "What's behind that question?"
2. Ask for an alternative positive behavior (APB). You might say, "You obviously disagree, Bill. Tell me, what would you do instead?"
3. Use the Feel, Felt, Found technique. For example, let's say a participant objects to your presentation saying, "You want us to spend $50,000 just to make this process easier on the workers?"

   You might respond, "I see you *feel* anxious about the expense. I *felt* that way too, until I *found* that the new process will reduce turnover. Reduced turnover will save us $25,000 in training costs, decrease bottlenecks, and reduce overtime and outside labor expenses to the tune of $10,000. Furthermore, when we send the work out the quality suffers and sometimes delivery schedules aren't met. I think we'll recoup the $50,000 in satisfied customers and new business due to our increased efficiency alone."

Controlling

In this context, "Controlling" means monitoring the results of your presentation. The final thirty seconds of your speech is a "Call to Action." Your call might include closing the sale, requesting approval, or making assignments. The appropriate follow-up action would be placing the order, submitting the paperwork for approval, or sending out minutes, respectively. In any case, you need to manage activities afterward to attain desired outcomes.

7
Written Communication

INTRODUCTION

Daily, members of organizations communicate in written form. These communications may include:

➢ Letters
➢ E-mails
➢ Job descriptions
➢ Formal business letters
➢ Proposals
➢ Reports
➢ Presentations
➢ White papers

In order to be well written, each of these documents requires at least a minimal amount of preparation, exploration, organization, composition, and revision.

Preparation involves establishing your objective, identifying your reader's needs, and determining the scope of the piece. The answers to these questions will determine whether the information should be communicated via a letter, e-mail, proposal, etc.

Exploration encompasses doing the appropriate research. You may need to go to the library, search the internet, conduct personal interviews, or have people complete written questionnaires.

Organization for written communication is not unlike that of the formal presentation explained in the previous chapter. Models include: compare or contrast, general to specific, order of importance, and so forth.

Composition means writing the first draft utilizing the GUIDE model.

Revision comprises checking for accuracy, unity, emphasis, word choice, sentence structure, and spelling.

Applying GUIDE to Business Writing:

*G*ather Information

Remember, gathering information means looking at what has happened historically. Since written communication is one-way, you will have to Give Information instead of gathering it. While it is possible to gather information in a letter, you would have to wait for a reply and the process would take at least one letter for each of the five steps of GUIDE.

A more appropriate use of this step would be to provide the historical context and content you believe is pertinent to your objective and to the reader.

*U*nderstand the Available Information

This step is about verifying what is known. In the written form, it means clarifying the purpose of the letter, memo, etc.

*I*nvestigate Alternatives

Instead of seeking ideas, offer alternatives you believe could address the objective and would be suitable to the recipients. I'd suggest at least three, all of which would be acceptable to you.

*D*ecide on the Best Course of Action, *D*evelop a Plan, and *D*o It

Propose the solution from the previous step you think would be the best alternative for handling the objective. Be sure to explain your rationale for choosing this particular alternative.

*E*valuate Progress and Results, *E*xpress Gratitude

This is the time to show gratitude, in advance, for the recipients' taking the action you have proposed.

Applying CARE to Business Writing:

Look for opportunities to use the CARE behaviors in your writing (see Appendix A for tips). If the audience knows you CARE, you'll increase your probability of success. In written communications, this requires anticipating the audience reaction and choosing the appropriate written words to convey one of the following:

Commit -   Giving and expecting dedication builds trust and involvement.

Affirm -   Showing acceptance of the individual as a person preserves esteem and a sense of security in the journey.

Recognize -   Praising a person's value, effort, contributions, or results builds esteem and confidence.

Empathize -   Demonstrating that you are listening shows that you understand the person's message and feelings.

Key Principles of Effective Writing

As you compose your written work, keep in mind some key principles of effective writing. They will help you write in a way that will simplify complexity, reduce uncertainty, and resolve conflict. In short, you'll be less likely to be misunderstood.

Active Voice

Voice refers to the arrangement of the sentence. The effective writer uses the following structure: Subject – Verb – Object. In active voice the subject acts upon the object. For instance, *I typed the memo.* In passive voice the object comes first, like this: *The memo was typed by me.* This became crystal clear to me when a professor told me to do a global search of my manuscript for "was" and "is" and replace them with the action verb.

Ize-ing and Wise-ing

I heard Edwin Newman speak at a national convention of the American Society for Training and Development. One of the most memorable parts of his speech occurred when he talked about ize-ing and wise-ing. To ize means to add "ize" to a word, like: politicize, scrutinize, strategize, optimize, personalize, finalize, etc. My personal favorite is when a colleague said, "We need to routinize all our training programs."

Wise-ing refers to the addition of "wise" at the end of a word. You can hear it frequently when listening to sports broadcasters. As in, "Derek Jeter is a great player, shortstop-wise."

My feeling is people do this because they think it makes them sound smarter. It does not. In fact, it makes them sound less intelligent. Avoid this mistake by simply using the basic sentence structure, "Derek Jeter plays shortstop well."

Keep Sentences Short

Usually the shorter the sentence the easier it is to understand. I'd suggest sentences should be less than fifteen words, but occasionally could go up to twenty.

Be Specific

This principle is particularly important in the Decide phase of GUIDE, therefore, I'm re-emphasizing that you should select the alternative that best matches the objective of your writing. Then ask:

> "Who needs to do what and by when to implement the solution?"

There may be other questions you'll want to ask to pin down the plan of action. Such as, how, why, and where; but who, what, and when are the most important.

Coherence Provides Clarity

A sentence is logical when all its parts contribute to one idea. For example, the position of the word "only" changes the meaning of the following sentences:

> Only she read the book *Lonesome Dove*. (No one else read it.)
> She only read the book *Lonesome Dove*. (She didn't annotate it.)
> She read only the book *Lonesome Dove*. (Not the screenplay.)
> She read the only book *Lonesome Dove*. (There was just one copy.)
> She read the book *Lonesome Dove* only. (She read no other book.)

Other types of modifiers can confuse the reader as well. Make sure you write what you intend. "We almost lost everything in the fire." is different than saying, "We lost almost everything in the fire."

Here's another. "With his tail spinning like a propeller, David took his dog for a walk." Is David's tail spinning? Of course not. It should read, "With his tail spinning like a propeller, the dog took David for a walk." Huh?

"Their" is Not a Singular Pronoun

If you are too young to remember chalk boards in classrooms, then you may need to watch the scene in Jaws where Quint drags his fingernails down said slate to get the City Council's attention. That unbelievably irritating sound, the one that makes the hair stand up on my neck, is what I hear when someone uses "their" as a singular pronoun.

It has become so pervasive that I hear teachers using it. Richard Bolles, author of the best-selling book *What Color is Your Parachute,* spends a full two pages in the preface of his book explaining why he has chosen to use poor grammar and language throughout the book. He apparently wants to be politically correct and not offend feminists who object to using "he" as a neutral pronoun. He says he wants to save *unnecessary correspondence* from unemployed English teachers. He wants to utilize a non-sexist style in his book.

As in, "No one in their right mind would use 'their' as a singular pronoun." The reason this bothers me so much is because the fix is so easy. Here are three ways to fix this sentence:

1. Change "No one" to "People"
2. Change "their" to "his" or "her," but please avoid "his/her"
3. Change "their" to an article "a," "an," or "the"

Choose the Appropriate Word

Just as there are different ways to lead, based upon the maturity level of the employee, there are different ways to write, based upon the education level of the audience. Word choice should be based upon what is appropriate for the situation.

If you are writing to the Board of Directors, you might write at a higher grade level than if you are writing to front line employees. Unfortunately, most adults read at an eighth grade level, as reported by the National Center for Education Statistics. So when in doubt, choose the simpler word. This usually means fewer syllables, less jargon, and informal rather than highly technical words. For instance, replace "termination of the illumination" with "turn out the lights."

Make Sentence Elements Parallel

Parallel construction means making words or phrases in a series or sequence match in grammatical structure.

For instance, "I like playing baseball, cooking dinner, and to read novels" lacks parallel construction. It should read, "I like playing baseball, cooking dinner, and reading novels" or "I like to play baseball, cook dinner, and read novels."

A Note on Writing E-mail

Avoid using e-mail if:

> ➢ Your message is confidential
> ➢ You are delivering unpleasant news
> ➢ There is a chance your message could be misunderstood
> ➢ You need an immediate response
> ➢ Your message is more than three paragraphs
> ➢ You need to involve several people in a discussion

8

One to One Communication

INTRODUCTION

An interpersonal conversation is a discussion between at least two people in which there is complexity, uncertainty, or conflict. Therefore, your goal is to simplify complexity, reduce uncertainty and resolve conflict which leads to better decisions and better relationships.

Examples of the type of conversations you might have include:

- ➤ Giving feedback to anyone about his behavior
- ➤ Evaluating a co-worker's performance
- ➤ Talking to a team member who is always tardy
- ➤ Confronting a colleague who is stealing supplies
- ➤ Working through an unfavorable performance review
- ➤ Voicing concern about someone's personal hygiene
- ➤ Correcting a serious employee performance problem
- ➤ Resolving a conflict between employees
- ➤ Firing an employee
- ➤ Investigating a complaint of harassment or discrimination on the job
- ➤ Assisting someone with personal problems that are effecting his work
- ➤ Discussing breach of ethics in the workplace

Throughout the remainder of this book, you will receive examples of how to handle these types of interpersonal conversations using GUIDE, CARE, and SPIN. You will see how GUIDE is used as a meeting agenda and the CARE behaviors are used as needed to maintain or enhance the relationship.

Applying GUIDE to Interpersonal Conversations:

Imagine that GUIDE is a road map and CARE is used to break through roadblocks. While the specific details may change depending upon the purpose of the discussion, the process remains the same.

Gather Information

Remember, gathering information means looking at what has happened historically. If your purpose is to delegate, you'll ask questions about the employee's past experiences pertaining to the specific assignment being delegated. If you're in a selection interview, you'll ask the applicant about past experiences pertaining to the critical job qualifications. If you want to correct a poor work habit, you'll ask questions about the cause of the problem. If you are conducting a performance review, you'll ask questions about how the associate reached a goal or failed to meet an expectation.

Once you feel you have all the facts, move to the next step.

Understand the Available Information

This step is about verifying what is known. My personal style is to summarize what I've heard in the Gather stage and ask, "Is that right?" or, "Have I missed anything?"

Investigate Alternatives

The future starts here. If your purpose is to delegate, you'll ask questions about ways to accomplish the specific assignment being delegated. If you're selecting a new associate, you'll ask members of the selection team which candidates are viable. If you want to correct a poor work habit, you'll ask how the employee proposes to solve the problem. If you are conducting a performance review, you'll ask the associate to set new goals for the coming year.

Once you feel you have explored all the alternatives, move to the next step.

Decide on the Best Course of Action, Develop a Plan, and Do It

This step is about solidifying the decision. My personal style is to ask the other person to summarize who, will do what, by when. I usually say something like, "Just to make sure we are both clear, why don't you tell me what we've agreed to today."

Once you feel there is agreement, set an appropriate follow-up date to review progress.

Evaluate Progress and Results, Express Gratitude

In most cases, you will evaluate the results during the follow-up meeting.

For now, focus on thanking the other party. If your purpose is to delegate, you'll express gratitude for the employee's willingness to take on the specific assignment being delegated. If you're selecting a new associate, you'll thank the candidates for their interest in the job. If you want to correct a poor work habit, you'll show confidence in the associate's ability to correct the situation. If you are conducting a performance review, you'll convey belief in the worker's ability to reach the new goals in the coming year.

Applying CARE to Interpersonal Conversations:

GUIDE is a model that can be applied to virtually any vital conversation. GUIDE is sequential. While it may be necessary to back track or use GUIDE in a loop fashion, it is most successful when followed in order.

CARE is not sequential. The CARE behaviors are to be used when necessary to overcome roadblocks, maintain a fragile relationship, or enhance another's self-esteem. The challenge in using CARE is to choose the correct behavior.

For instance, if I begin a conversation and the employee reacts defensively, I need to affirm. People defend when they feel attacked; therefore, self-esteem needs to be maintained. If the person reacts with anger, I need to show empathy. I'll not be able to continue with the agenda until I reduce or eliminate the interfering emotion. If the person seems disengaged, I need to seek commitment.

Use of the CARE behaviors is most frequently a function of the employee's reaction.

Together GUIDE and CARE help people successfully accomplish tasks in the context of positive, trusting, and reinforcing relationships. Use the form on the following page to plan your discussions.

Discussion GUIDE

*G*ather information
Seek staff input 1st   Offer your input 2nd   Facts, data, stats, dates, projects
worked on/completed.... Focus on job not the person

Commit
Affirm
Recognize
Empathize

*U*nderstand the available information
You believe...   You feel...   Agree or agree to disagree?   Summarize
Check for understanding (yours & theirs)

*I*nvestigate alternatives
"What ideas do you have about...?"   Use or build on staff ideas when possible   Offer own ideas last

*D*ecide on the best course of action, Develop a plan, and Do it
Who, what, when, where, why, how

Set follow-up dates/times

*E*valuate progress and results, Express gratitude
"Thanks for meeting with me today. I appreciate your input. You're a valuable contributor... I found
this helpful. Did this meet your expectations? "

Positive Model: Interpersonal Conversation

Most interpersonal conversations using the GUIDE process can be conducted in ten to twenty minutes. Occasionally they may take less time if the subject is simple, there is only one item on the agenda, or the other person is particularly cooperative. If there are many items on the agenda as is the case with a performance review, the discussion may take an hour or longer. GUIDE can also be used in problem-solving meetings with several participants. Obviously, the more people in the meeting the longer it will take.

Here is an example of what might happen if you were coaching an employee to plan for the next team retreat.

Gather information:

> **Leader** – Hi Miles, I'm so happy that you have volunteered to plan the next team retreat. I am committed to helping you succeed with this project, so I thought we should get together to discuss it. Why don't we start with you telling me what you have done so far?
>
> **Miles** – Well, I haven't done much yet. I put together this list of things to do, that's about it.
>
> **Leader** – This is a great start. You have thought of transportation, lodging, food, and activities. Now we just have to get specific.
>
> **Miles** – What do you mean?
>
> **Leader** – Well, you know you have to schedule the lodging. Have you thought about which location might suit our needs best?
>
> **Miles** – I see what you mean now.

Understand the available information:

> **Leader** – So we have a "To DO" list, which gives the four general categories of the plan. Right?
>
> **Miles** – Right.

Investigate alternatives:

> **Leader** – Why don't we take each category and do a little brainstorming. You want to start with lodging?
>
> **Miles** – Okay, I was thinking about that resort in Boerne. They have a great restaurant, sleeping accommodations, leisure activities, and space for us to meet.

Leader – Miles, that is a good one. Any others?

Miles – Well, there's a camp just outside of Victoria.

Leader – There's also one up near Wichita Falls.

(This continues until they have completed the brainstorming and reduced the list for each category)

Decide on the best course of action, Develop a plan, Do it:

Leader – Okay, Miles, based upon what we've discussed why don't you summarize what you'll do next.

Miles – I'm going to do three things. First, I'll develop an action plan with deadlines and allocate resources. Then, I'll contact everyone involved to confirm the commitment to the plan. Finally, I'll make the appropriate reservations.

Leader – When do you think you can complete the plan?

Miles – By the end of the week.

Leader – That sounds perfect. Why don't you show me your plan before you move to step two.

Miles – I will.

Evaluate progress and results, Express gratitude:

Leader – Thanks for your help on this project, Miles. I'm confident that if you follow the steps we outlined today, you will be very successful.

Section Three

Selecting and Developing Organizational Talent

9

Selecting Talent

INTRODUCTION

Selection Interviewing is a complex and time consuming process. This chapter covers the following behavioral competency:

Selecting Talent – The process of attracting potential employees and choosing the best candidate based upon extensive data collection. This includes:

> ➤ Identifying the most critical job qualifications
> ➤ Planning and consistently applying a step-by-step procedure
> ➤ Practicing effective interviewing skills
> ➤ Creating a positive impression

This chapter will help you make the most of your time and increase the likelihood of your organization hiring individuals who are qualified to do the job.

The objective of effective interviewing is to hire people who have the necessary skills, knowledge, and desire to do a specific job. It is important to ensure that you interview for all three elements.

The benefits of thoroughly interviewing for all three elements are to:

> ➤ Improve Productivity
> ➤ Increase Job Satisfaction
> ➤ Retain Qualified People
> ➤ Increase Organizational Effectiveness

In order to reap these benefits, it is important to use effective interviewing strategies. The following represent the most important elements:

> ➤ Identify the most critical job qualifications
> ➤ Plan and consistently apply a step-by-step procedure
> ➤ Practice effective interviewing skills
> ➤ Create a positive impression

Applying GUIDE as a Selection Process

Gather Information

This is where the selection interviews will take place. Interviewers will use SPIN to seek information about each applicant's past behavior in order to prove that the candidate can or cannot do the job.

Understand the Available Information

This step is about verifying what is known. You might want to contact references to confirm that the applicant actually was successful in previous jobs. The questions will be nearly identical to the ones used with the applicant.

Investigate Alternatives

At this step, the interview team will conduct an integration meeting using a criteria-based method. In this case, the criteria will be the behavioral competencies for the job.

Decide on the Best Course of Action, Develop a Plan, and Do It

Select the best candidate by doing another criteria-based decision in which the alternatives are the candidates that made the final cut.

Evaluate Progress and Results, Express Gratitude

Full evaluation of the new hire will have to wait until the person's results can be documented. In the meantime treat all applicants with CARE.

IDENTIFY THE MOST CRITICAL JOB QUALIFICATIONS

A detailed study of the requirements necessary to effectively complete a job should be done prior to any interviewing process. This job analysis should focus on behavior that is required of the applicant.

Information can be collected from a variety of sources for this study. For example, you might want to examine the person's job description, interview incumbents, and interview managers or supervisors who have knowledge of what would make an applicant successful or unsuccessful in the job. It is important to focus on behavior not responsibility.

The difference is that a behavior is what a person does in a given situation; a responsibility is what a person is accountable for.

Therefore, in identifying the most critical job qualifications, you are trying to describe how a successful worker would conduct himself in a particular job.

PLAN AND CONSISTENTLY APPLY A STEP-BY-STEP PROCEDURE

The process used from initial recruiting through the final hiring decision should be planned thoroughly and applied consistently for each applicant of a given job. This will ensure that each applicant is treated fairly and that the hiring process is efficient.

In planning the process, it is important to keep in mind such things as advertising, recruiting, telephone screening, the number of interviews necessary, and reference checks. Medical exams and assessment activities should also be planned if your organization requires them.

Regardless of which of these components are used, it is essential to have all applicants go through the same process in virtually the same order.

When planning the process, effective managers have more expensive elements occur toward the end of the process. They ensure that there is full coverage of the critical job qualifications, do not overlap questions, and share the responsibility for giving information to the candidates.

Although in-depth information can be collected in a variety of ways, there should be at least two face-to-face interviews. It is better to involve a third person in collecting data in some way so that three individuals share the hiring decision.

PRACTICE EFFECTIVE INTERVIEWING SKILLS

The skills most needed for conducting an effective interview include:

- ➤ A friendly opening
- ➤ Gathering general information about the applicant's background
- ➤ Asking questions that will elicit behavior associated with the most critical job qualifications
- ➤ Asking follow-up questions that will encourage the candidate to offer complete information
- ➤ Controlling the pace of the interview
- ➤ Closing the interview and answering questions

A Friendly Opening

When a person opens an interview, it is appropriate to be social, offer something to drink, or compliment the person's resume.

Gathering General Information

Most interviews begin with a discussion of the background information. The interviewer fills in any gaps in the resume or application form, asking several general questions.

The purpose of this general information is to determine where the person might have had experiences that would be similar to the available position. This opening should not be longer than 5 to 7 minutes.

Asking Questions About Critical Job Qualifications

The majority of time in the interview is spent asking specific questions. The questions should focus on the person's behavior in previous positions relative to the job qualifications of the open position.

Each interviewer is responsible for collecting data on three to five qualifications. By spending approximately 5 minutes per qualification, the body of the interview would last from 15 to 25 minutes.

Asking Follow-Up Questions

The interviewer must listen carefully to the answers and be prepared to ask follow-up questions designed to clearly understand the examples being offered by the applicant.

Controlling the Pace

The pace of the interview must be controlled by the interviewer. This may require intervening to encourage the applicant to provide more or less detail.

Closing the Interview and Answering Questions

Before closing the interview, the interviewer should allow ample time (10 to 15 minutes) to answer the applicant's questions. The applicant will most likely want to know information about the job responsibilities, reporting relationships, work hours, salary and benefits, and training and development.

The applicant may also want to know information about the organization's history, number of employees, major services, and reputation. The interviewer should be knowledgeable in all of these areas.

CREATE A POSITIVE IMPRESSION

The interviewing process is a two-way street. Not only do you want to gather enough information about the applicant's ability to handle the job, you also want to impress the candidate with the quality of the work environment or other attributes of joining the organization. This is important for two reasons: first, you don't want to lose a qualified applicant because of a less than favorable impression of our organization; and second, each applicant is a potential customer and even though you may not offer every applicant a job, you want them all to leave feeling they were given a fair chance.

There are four things to keep in mind:

> ➢ Before the interview, develop a checklist and interviewing schedule
> ➢ During the interview, maintain the applicant's dignity
> ➢ Sell the organization
> ➢ Follow-up promptly

There is nothing worse, from the applicant's point of view, than waiting in a reception area for hours. Be sure to have a schedule of interviews and plan for filler activities between assignments or in the event that a schedule does go off track. You might also want to assign the applicant a host or hostess.

The most important skill to creating a positive impression is to maintain the applicant's dignity. This can be done by complementing effective examples or responding in an empathetic fashion. Both of these show acceptance of the applicant in what can be a very stressful situation.

Selling the organization means providing information the applicant needs and wants. Showing the applicant specific value of his or her coming to work for this company will go a long way in influencing the applicant's decision. The focus here is on what the company will do for the applicant not what the applicant will do for the company.

Finally, the interviewer should follow-up promptly. If you say you will notify the applicant of your decision by next Tuesday, do it.

Let's explore the elements of Selecting Talent in more detail.

EXPLORING FREQUENT DIFFICULTIES

More often than not, hiring decisions result in turnover, absenteeism, poor job quality or less than acceptable quantity. These decisions affect the effectiveness of your entire work group. The reasons for these problems are the result of correctable mistakes.

Following are several of the most frequent difficulties that managers experience:

> ➢ Not all job qualifications are explored
> ➢ Managers ask the same questions
> ➢ Interviewer plays amateur psychiatrist
> ➢ Decisions made based upon likes and dislikes
> ➢ Managers tend to lower standards if position is vacant too long
> ➢ No standard step-by-step procedures

UNDERSTANDING EFFECTIVE INTERVIEWING STRATEGIES

This section covers the four most important elements to effective selection. They are:

- ➤ Identify the most critical job qualifications
- ➤ Plan and consistently apply a step-by-step procedure
- ➤ Practice effective interviewing skills
- ➤ Create a positive impression

Identify the Most Critical Job Qualifications

When identifying the job qualifications, decide what behavior an applicant must exhibit to be successful in the job. Don't look for all behaviors but rather the six to ten without which the applicant would certainly fail (see Defining Job Qualifications in Chapter 3). It is important for us to understand what a behavior is.

Example:

A courier is expected to deliver specimens to a lab in time for tests to be reliable. His behavior could be that he is constantly late.

If hiring for a courier, one of the qualifications might be planning ability. The label "planning" would indicate an ability to chart his route in order to meet time schedules.

The purpose of focusing on behavior is to find out how a person conducts himself within his area of responsibility.

What are the behaviors that would be most crucial to the job of Courier?

- ➤ Ability to learn
- ➤ Communication
- ➤ Sensitivity to customers
- ➤ Decision-making ability
- ➤ Tolerance for stress
- ➤ Planning
- ➤ Work safety
- ➤ Decisiveness
- ➤ Attention to detail

In addition to these skill areas, the interviewer *must* collect data on two *mandatory* qualifications.

- ➤ Technical proficiency
- ➤ Desire to do this work

Technical proficiency is important to always have on the list of qualifications because every job requires a minimum level of technical expertise. A courier must have the ability to drive. A secretary must type X number of words per minute without error. A salesman must have a minimum level of product knowledge to be successful. A medical technologist must understand how to run the diagnostic tests for quality of service.

Without desire to do this work, there is no guarantee that the newly hired employee will do what is expected. It is important to make a distinction between desire to work and desire to do *this* work. It is quite possible to interview someone who just wants a job and seems willing to take any responsibility. You are looking for someone who derives job satisfaction from doing the tasks and assignments required of this job. Therefore, there is a match or "fit."

Plan and Consistently Apply a Step-By-Step Procedure

Although each organization might have its own system, all selection processes follow a basic pattern like the one shown below:

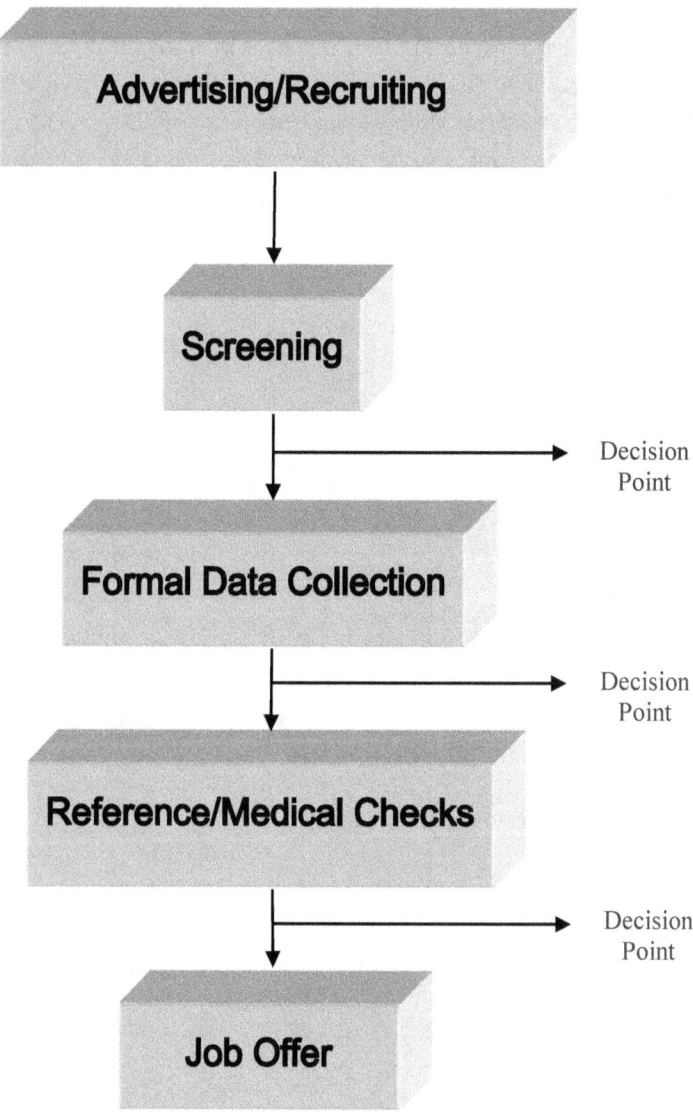

Practice Effective Interviewing Skills

Well worded questions will encourage an applicant to discuss work related experiences. It is the interviewer's responsibility to focus on behavior, meaning the actions a person has taken in a particular situation. The interviewer will want to word the questions in the past tense.

Example:

"What kinds of problems have you solved recently?"

"What were some of the best ideas you tried but failed to sell to a supervisor?"

"How did you decide on top priorities when scheduling your time?"

| SPIN |
| Situation |
| Performance |
| Impact |
| Next Time |
| |
| Specific and |
| Behavioral |

These questions are a starting point. The interviewer will need to follow-up to make sure the information is complete and clear. Here's an example of how an interview might progress:

Interviewer: "How did you decide on top priorities when scheduling your time?"

Applicant: "I decide which task is the most urgent and do it."

Interviewer: "Could you describe a recent day in which you had many things to do?"

Applicant: "I had a special report that was due and I also had to complete a financial report."

Interviewer: "How did you decide which one was more urgent?"

Applicant: "The special report had an earlier deadline and I knew I had a few more days to complete the financial report."

Interviewer: "How did you know what the deadline was?"

Applicant: "The financial report is due on the 15th of every month, but the special report was needed within two days."

Interviewer: "What was the outcome?"

Applicant: "I finished the special report before it was needed and used the extra time to complete the financial report by the 15th."

In this example, the interviewer used SPIN questions to get a complete behavioral example. He was able to determine that the applicant looked for the most recent deadline and worked on the project that was needed first. Had the interviewer stopped with the first question, no evidence of effective planning would have been discovered.

Notice the wording of the Situation question, "Could you describe a recent day in which you had many things to do?" The interviewer wants the applicant to describe a specific incident within a reasonable time frame. If the example happened ten years ago, it would be less reliable than if it happened three months ago.

The most significant questions are related to Performance. Such as, "How did you decide which one was more urgent?" This question is designed to ascertain the thinking process the applicant used. In other areas the questions would be about the actions the person took. Such as, "What did you do in that situation?"

To ensure a complete behavioral example the interviewer must find out the Impact of the technique used, "What was the outcome?" The impact tells us whether the Performance was effective or not.

Questions related to Next Time are rare, but might be used if the Impact or Performance were negative. The interviewer could ask, "Has anything similar happened since then?" If so, ask, "What did you do the Next Time?"

In addition, the interviewer should avoid asking leading or hypothetical questions. In the previous example, it would have been easy for the interviewer to ask a leading question like, "Were you able to complete both projects?" This would have led the applicant to respond with an answer beneficial to the quest of the job; such as, "Absolutely."

Hypothetical questions are ineffective because the applicant can fake a response. An example of a hypothetical question would be, "If you were given two projects with the same deadline, how would you decide which to do first?"

By asking the future oriented question, the applicant can respond with a theoretical or textbook type answer. This may be how the person *might* behave but doesn't describe how the person *has* behaved in the past which makes it less predictive of job success. Good behavioral questions require the applicant to describe past performance not feelings, opinions, or theories.

Follow-Up Questions

In order to be certain that the applicant isn't embellishing, three things need to be discovered.

> ➤ **S - Why The Person Behaved**. The behavior could be a result of a job responsibility or a reaction to some situational factor.
> ➤ **P - The Specific Actions Taken**. The behavior could be something said or done.
> ➤ **I - The Effect of the Behavior**. The behavior could have resulted in a positive or negative outcome.

If any of the three components is missing, you have an incomplete example. The best way to determine if you have a complete or incomplete example is to keep the SPIN acronym in mind. Each of the first three components of SPIN represent the previous elements. Namely:

Situation = why the person behaved
Performance = the specific actions taken
Impact = the effect of the behavior
Next Time = use sparing

In addition to the complete response, the interviewer should be aware of hypothetical answers. Even when the initial question is asked perfectly, the applicant might give a textbook type answer. This type of theoretical response may indicate the person has some knowledge but does not indicate how that knowledge was applied.

Create a Positive Impression

There are opportunities to create a positive impression throughout the entire selection process. Before, during and after the interview the applicant will be generating perceptions of the company, you and the work environment. It is important that these be positive perceptions.

You will want to ensure that the applicant has a schedule with the names and titles of the assigned interviewers. There should be someone assigned as the key contact. Applicants appreciate a home base between interviews with company literature or other reading material.

Some of the things that are most important to prepare for before the interview include:

> ➤ Travel & lodging information
> ➤ Home base

> An interview schedule
> A key contact

During the interview, the best way to create a positive impression is by maintaining the applicant's dignity. All applicants are vulnerable in an interview situation. This creates stress because the applicant does not want to appear unqualified. The applicant might be thinking:

> Do I look right?
> Am I making a good impression?
> Did I answer that question correctly?

The interviewer needs to be aware of these unasked questions. By complementing a person's appearance, experience or response, you maintain the applicant's dignity. If the response is negative information, it might be more appropriate to empathize or rationalize.

Here are some examples:

> "That was a clever way of handling the situation."
> "That's exactly the kind of information I am looking for."
> "I can understand why you might have felt pressured in that situation."
> "Everybody has made a mistake like that."

Maintaining an applicant's dignity is an important interviewing skill. In the following examples, note how the interviewer might maintain the applicant's dignity by complementing, empathizing or rationalizing.

Applicant: "I am great at organizing my time."

Interviewer: "That's an important skill. I can see that you're proud of your ability."

Applicant: "I didn't like dealing with Mr. Moreno, he was always so hostile."

Interviewer: "That can be frustrating."

Applicant: "Dave always worked on Saturday and frequently damaged my computer disks."

Interviewer: "That must have been terribly irritating."

Applicant: "Procrastination is my only fault, but I work best under pressure."

Interviewer: "We all have similar concerns."

Applicant: "The rate on my typing test was 114 words per minute with 3 errors."

Interviewer: "That's an outstanding speed."

After you have asked the applicant questions on all assigned qualifications, you will want to give the applicant the opportunity to ask you questions about the job. This will give you the opportunity to sell the organization.

Following are some examples of value statements you might use:

- ➢ "We have a company suggestion box and the employee recommending the most cost effective improvement is given a bonus."
- ➢ "We offer van pooling."
- ➢ "There is dental coverage in the health plan."
- ➢ "The health club offers reduced memberships for our employees."

LEGALESE

Title VII of the Civil Rights Act of 1964 prohibits discrimination based upon race, color, religion, sex, or national origin in all employment practices. This includes hiring, firing, promotion, compensation, and any other conditions of employment.

The Equal Employment Opportunity Commission (EEOC) was created to administer Title VII. Following are EEOC guidelines on subjects you cannot ask about during an employment interview:

- ➢ Age
- ➢ Race
- ➢ National origin
- ➢ Religion
- ➢ Marital status
- ➢ Number of dependents
- ➢ Child care
- ➢ Housing
- ➢ Arrest record
- ➢ Health status
- ➢ Type of military discharge
- ➢ Willingness to work weekends
- ➢ Any other information from minority or female applicants not routinely asked of white or male applicants

On the following page is a list of all the questions you *can* ask.

ANY JOB RELATED QUESTION

INTERVIEW GUIDE

A typical interviewing guide contains three sections: the Opening, the Behavioral Questions and the Closing. The Behavioral Questions section includes from five to eight pages that represent the job qualifications that are assigned to the interviewer.

On a three-person team, there will be overlap which means each person on the team will ask different questions about the top three competencies. Two people on the team will be assigned questions about the middle priority competencies and each person on the team will be assigned one of the lowest priority competencies.

On each page of an Interview Guide you are striving to get at least three behavioral examples for the job qualifications you are assigned. A complete behavioral example must include all three components: Situation, Performance and Impact. If information is missing from any of the three components, you must ask a follow-up question to complete the illustration of the applicant's experience.

The Opening

To start an interview, use these guidelines:

➤ Greet the applicant, being appropriately sociable
➤ Explain the purpose of the interview
➤ Describe the interview plan
➤ Explain that you will be taking notes
➤ Review background information

The Behavioral Questions

Then move to the main part of the interview to explore specific accomplishments in more detail. Samples from an actual Interview Guide are shown on the following three pages. In these examples, the job you would be interviewing for is a Customer Service Representative.

The Closing

When you have covered all assigned job qualifications, allow the applicant to ask questions. Then review your assigned information about the company and close the interview by describing the next steps, and thank the applicant for the opportunity to get to know him better.

Desire To Do This Work – Derives satisfaction and job fulfillment from dealing with customers, meeting their needs and handling their concerns.

1. What did you like best about your job at ___*the Hotel*___?

2. What did you like least about your job at ___*the Hotel*___?

3. Why did you leave that position?

Situation	Performance	Impact
Worked as Bell Hop	*Liked interacting with the guests*	*Would get better tips*

Customer Service Orientation – Proactively develops customer relationships, makes efforts to listen to and understand the customer, and anticipates and provides solutions to customer needs.

1. Tell me about the most you've ever done to try to satisfy a particular customer?

2. Sooner or later, we all have to deal with a customer who makes unreasonable demands. Think of a time when you had to handle an unreasonable request. What did you do?

3. Occasionally, we wish we could have handled a customer better. Tell me about a recent interaction you wish you would have handled differently.

Situation	Performance	Impact
Call with demanding prospect threatening to change vendors	*Remained calm, offered to contact AE and report back same day*	*Prospect thanked me for helping him*

Teamwork – Works effectively with a work group or those outside the formal line of authority (e.g. peers, senior managers, or others outside the department) to accomplish organizational goals.

1. Describe a situation when you were able to help out a peer or team member?

2. Interacting with others can be challenging at times. Describe a situation when you wished you'd acted differently with someone at work. What happened?

3. Tell me about one of the toughest teams you've had to work with. What made it difficult? What did you do?

Situation	Performance	Impact
Participated in a task force	*Complained about wasted time and no good ideas*	*Behavior didn't change and morale dropped*

COMPETENCE ANALYSIS

Once the `interview is completed the interviewer should examine notes on the interview guide. You are looking for evidence of the candidate's competence. This evidence needs to be in the form of a complete behavior, including the following three elements:

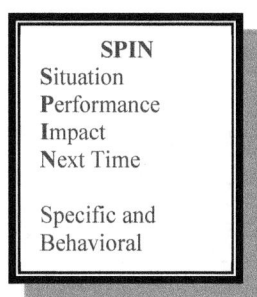

> **S - Why the Person Behaved**. The behavior could be a result of a job responsibility or a reaction to some situational factor.
> **P - The Specific Actions Taken**. The behavior could be something said or done.
> **I - The Effect of the Behavior**. The behavior could have resulted in a positive or negative outcome.

SPIN
Situation
Performance
Impact
Next Time

Specific and
Behavioral

Once you have identified a complete behavioral example, you will need to correctly identify which of the competencies it most closely matches.

For example if the candidate said:

"I was part of the management training program at Colgate-Palmolive. They had me work in many different departments to learn about all aspects of the company. I worked on an Action Research Team in the toothpaste manufacturing plant, helped design a marketing campaign, and prepared P & L statements in the Financial Planning Department. They said I had the highest scores of any of the trainees."

Then you would write "Adaptability" next to that example in your notes. You should also note if the example was effective (+) or ineffective (-) relative to the position in question.

Finally, you will need to evaluate each competency based upon the number, pertinence, and recency of the examples using the following key:

> **B** - Below the job requirements
> **L** - Less than acceptable
> **S** - Satisfactory
> **M** - More than acceptable
> **E** - Exceeds the job requirements

Criteria-Based Decision Making

Each candidate should be interviewed by at least three interviewers. After all interviews have been completed the interview team must meet to compare notes and agree on a consensus rating for each competency evaluated.

The first step is to post individual ratings on a flip chart, white board, or integration sheet as follows:

Candidate #1	Interviewer #1	Interviewer #2	Interviewer #3	Consensus
Customer Service Orientation	M	S	M	
Initiative	B	S		
Adaptability	M		E	
Quality Orientation		L	S	
Teamwork		E	S	
Communication	L	S	M	
Work Pace	M		L	
Desire to Do This Work	L	S		

Then each interviewer explains the rationale for the rating by using the behavioral evidence collected. One by one a consensus rating is established for each competency. The hiring decision is based upon comparing the consensus ratings among all candidates who were interviewed.

10

Orienting New Hires

INTRODUCTION

Once you have hired a new employee, you will want to orient the associate to the company, department, and job. This chapter covers the following behavioral competency:

Orienting New Hires – The process of making the newly hired employee feel welcome by:

- ➢ Putting the new employee at ease
- ➢ Talking about how the candidate did during the interview process and why you hired this person
- ➢ Providing information on the company history, day-to-day operations, policies, etc.
- ➢ Describing what you would like the employee to work on first
- ➢ Expressing pleasure that the employee has joined your work group

What Is Orienting?

The dictionary defines orient this way:

to familiarize (a person) with new surroundings or circumstances, or the like:

Lectures designed to orient the new students.

Why Do We Orient?

The purpose of orienting the new employee is to make that person comfortable. In many cases, coming to a new job with unfamiliar surroundings can make a person feel anxiety. In order to get the best work from a new employee, you'll want to reduce the stress as best you can.

Another reason for orienting the employee is to get that person productive as soon as possible. The sooner you get the employee producing, the sooner you are making money.

One of the reasons employees leave companies is because they don't feel valued. Orienting them to the new job ensures them that you CARE about their success.

There is a management axiom about time that says, *the time you spend now will save time later*. An effective orientation will set the employee up for success.

Learning about corporate values, rules and regulations, and specific job expectations will make the new person feel welcome, aware, and part of the team.

How Do We Orient?

Orienting the new employee involves one or more discussions between the supervisor and the new hire. The main purpose of meeting is to make the new employee feel welcome and comfortable with others in the work group. This initial orientation should provide the new employee with six types of information:

> ➤ Information about the day-to-day operations (location of restrooms, copy room, supply closet, etc.)
> ➤ A description of the organization's history, purpose, products and services, and how the employee's job contributes to the overall goals of the organization
> ➤ The organization's policies and procedures, work rules, and employee benefits
> ➤ Information about the interview process (review the behavioral competencies and scores given, especially if there are any areas that require training)
> ➤ Review the employee's position description and establish the performance expectations
> ➤ Provide Job Procedure Worksheets or other job aids

The time you spend with the employee should be targeted with goals regarding the things to cover. You'll want to make the first day a celebration. You might want to involve the family in a tour of the facility. Prepare an assignment to make sure the new person is productive on the first day. Don't rush through it. The orientation may take all day, so allow enough time to do it right.

The Process

Step 1 — Put the new employee at ease by being appropriately sociable.

Step 2 — Review the position description and talk about how the candidate did during the interview process. Provide feedback as necessary and describe any training you'd like to schedule.

Step 3 — Ask for questions and answer them directly. Provide information on the company history, day-to-day operations, policies, etc.

Step 4 — Describe what you would like the employee to work on first and how the employee should get help.

Step 5 — Express pleasure that the employee has joined your work group and confidence that the employee will do well in the new job.

Applying GUIDE to Orienting the New Employee

*G*ather Information

Start with a grand welcome. In this discussion, most of the information will be given rather than gathered. The challenge is to look for opportunities to engage the employee. At least 10% of the time check for understanding by asking questions like, "What do you think about that?" "What questions does that raise?"

*U*nderstand the Available Information

This step is more of a transition into the next step. You might want to ask the employee to summarize understanding or use a procedural suggestion like, "Why don't we move on to...."

*I*nvestigate Alternatives

This is the crux of the meeting. You'll want to take the employee on a tour, go over job expectation, provide information on the company history, day-to-day operations, policies, etc.

*D*ecide on the Best Course of Action, *D*evelop a Plan, and *D*o It

Describe what you would like the employee to work on first and how the employee should get help.

*E*valuate Progress and Results, *E*xpress Gratitude

Express pleasure that the employee has joined your work group and confidence that the employee will do well in the new job.

Positive Model: Orienting the New Employee

Orienting the new employee is one of the most neglected functions in many organizations. Dumping an employee handbook or company brochures on the new hire doesn't cut it. Here is a sample of what might happen during this type of discussion for a Customer Service Representative.

Gather information:

> **Leader** – Judith, welcome to TGC. I'm very excited about working with you. I have set aside the entire morning so we can get acquainted. I will try to answer any questions you may have and get you oriented to your new surroundings. This discussion will help you understand the interview process and why we selected you over other candidates. We'll also talk about the job and who might help you the most.

> **Judith** – That sounds great.

> **Leader** – Okay, let's start with the position description (hands her a copy). Our company utilizes self-directed work teams, which means there are no supervisors. Technically, everyone reports to the Plant Director. There are Team Coaches who are assigned to three or four teams each. Your coach's name is Brendan. I'll introduce you and he'll take you to lunch so the two of you can start getting to know each other. Brendan will explain his role and how the two of you will work together. He'll also be your first contact if you need help.

> **Judith** – I've never worked on a self-directed team.

> **Leader** – That may make you feel a little hesitant or tense, but Brendan will ease you into it. We believe they improve quality, productivity, and service which, of course, you are a big part.

> **Judith** – Well, it sounds like an adventure.

> **Leader** – Let me show you the competencies (points to the second page). All the candidates were questioned about these eight areas. You can see that Customer Service Orientation is right at the top of the list. We thought you provided many examples of your ability in this area. These competencies are the way we manage every aspect of your career with TGC.

> **Judith** – What do you mean?

Leader – We use them in the selection process, the performance management process, the career development process, and the evaluation process. You'll be seeing these competencies come up nearly every day.

(The leader continues to talk about the competencies until all are covered)

Leader – Next, let's talk about the company…

(The leader discusses the company's history, products, corporate goals, etc.)

Leader – So, you can see that you play an important role here at TGC. Our customers will depend upon your service.

Judith – That makes me feel good.

(The leader continues to provide information that Judith will find useful)

Understand the available information:

Leader – Do you have any particular questions you'd like me to answer now?

Judith – Where will I be working?

Leader – Why don't I take you on a tour?

Investigate alternatives:

(The leader shows Judith her work station, copy room, supply closet, etc.)

Leader – This afternoon you can check out what you have at your work station. If you'll make a list of what you need, I'll be happy to get it for you.

Judith – Okay, that will be great.

Leader – One of our corporate goals is to increase our customer satisfaction. In fact, we want more than satisfaction; we want customer delight. Do you have any ideas on how to achieve that?

Judith – Well, yes, I believe that every person has positive intentions. Even when a customer calls and is angry or behaves in less than acceptable ways, I assume he had reasons that made sense at the time. If I can get him to explain the reasons or what his needs are, then I can explore unconditionally constructive strategies to a win-win outcome.

Leader – That sounds interesting. What do you mean by unconditionally constructive strategies?

Judith – It doesn't do any good to argue back or take a stand; so, no matter how rude the customer is, I try to move the conversation to a positive place. You know, toward a mutually acceptable outcome.

Leader – Sounds like you've had quite a bit of experience with that strategy.

Judith – I have. If you like, I could put together a short training program for all the CSRs.

Leader – Okay, that might be helpful. After you are settled in, let's discuss that in more detail.

Judith – I'll look forward to it.

(The leader may wish to continue this line of questioning to involve the new employee in job relevant issues and hint at performance expectations)

Decide on the best course of action, Develop a plan, and Do it:

Leader – Okay, Judith, why don't we go over to meet Brendan?

Judith – Sounds good.

Leader – Brendan will ask you to do some work this afternoon, probably to start learning about our products and which customer issues come up most often.

Judith – That would be a good place to start.

Leader – Ultimately, I will be the one who conducts your performance appraisal, so it will be important for us to agree on your performance expectations. I'd like to schedule a meeting to do that on Wednesday afternoon at three. Will that work for you?

Judith – Absolutely.

Leader – That sounds perfect. Brendan will give you some preparatory work to do, so you'll be ready for the meeting.

Judith – I'll be ready.

Evaluate progress and results, Express gratitude:

Leader – I think you are going to be a wonderful addition to our team, Judith. I'm confident that you will be very successful. I look forward to our meeting on Wednesday.

11

Training on Job Skills

———————— ✳ ————————

INTRODUCTION

Soon after hiring a new employee, you will want to train the associate on job skills. This may be because the employee was rated less than acceptable during the interview or your company has a very particular way of handling this job. This chapter covers the following behavioral competency:

Training on Job Skills – The process of teaching a new employee how to do the work as part of the actual work shift. The process requires these four steps:

1. Describe the work to be done
2. Demonstrate the operation
3. Have the employee practice with feedback
4. Have the employee apply the skills alone

What is Training on Job Skills?

The dictionary defines training this way:

the education, instruction, or discipline of a person or thing that is being trained:

He's in training for the Olympics.

Why Do We Train On The Job?

The purpose of training the new employee is to make that person capable. In most cases, the new employee was hired because of acceptable ratings during the interview process. It is possible for a person to be hired with one or more unacceptable ratings, especially in a trainable dimension. Offering to spend the time training on a new job will enhance the new employee's morale.

Another reason for training the employee is to get that person productive as soon as possible. The sooner you get the employee producing to expected levels, the better for your output goals.

It's also a way for you to model professionalism. Employees appreciate the effort of a competent boss.

As mentioned in Orienting the New Employee, *the time you spend now will save time later*. Effective training will set the employee up for success and reduce startup costs.

How Do We Train?

Training on Job Skills was originally called Job Instruction Training (JIT) and in recent years referred to as On-the-Job Training (OJT). This type of training focuses on the acquisition of skills within the work environment under normal working conditions. The intention is for employees to acquire both general skills that they can transfer from one job to another and specific skills that are unique to a particular job. When Training on Job Skills, include four steps:

1. Vocal and written instruction
2. Demonstration and observation
3. Hands-on practice with feedback
4. Application of the skills on the job

The Process

One of the first structured on-the-job training programs was launched during World War I in the shipbuilding industry by Charles "Skipper" R. Allen, who based the program on the ideas of the psychologist Johann Friedrich Herbart. Allen sought to make training more efficient by having trainees undergo four steps:

1. Prepare: Put the worker at ease. Find out what he already knows. Enthusiastically tell the person what is required in the task and why it's required.

2. Present: Show how to do the job yourself, emphasizing key points.

3. Practice: Have the employee try the skill. Provide feedback to reinforce what was done correctly or improve anything done incorrectly.

4. Produce: Let the employee perform the required tasks. Check back periodically to ensure no significant problems.

Applying GUIDE to Training on Job Skills

Gather Information

In this discussion most of the information you will gather will pertain to the employee's past experience related to the job to be trained. Ask questions like, "How did you do this at your last job?" "What system did you use?" "When was the last time you did this kind of work?"

This would be a good time to give a written step-by-step procedure to the employee and explain the process thoroughly.

Understand the Available Information

In this step you'll want to summarize your understanding of what the employee already knows.

Investigate Alternatives

At this stage you should do the job yourself, pointing out any keys to success. Then, have the employee try out the techniques you just modeled. Provide feedback as the practice session continues. Allow the person to practice until it appears the skills are being performed as expected.

Decide on the Best Course of Action, Develop a Plan, and Do It

Let the employee work alone on the project. Check back with the employee in a reasonable period of time to see how it's going. Also suggest the employee should contact you if help is needed.

Evaluate Progress and Results, Express Gratitude

Express confidence that the employee will do well executing the new job.

Positive Model: Training on Job Skills

Training on Job Skills is one of best ways to help a newly hired employee get comfortable with general or specific skills needed in the job. Here is a sample of what might happen during this type of discussion for a Customer Service Representative.

Gather information:

> **Leader** – Judith, today I want to show you how to access and recognize customer information on your PC. This is something you'll be doing each and every day, so it's an important part of your job. Plus, you'll need to get proficient at it so you can get into a customer's file quickly. What kind of database did you use in your previous job?
>
> **Judith** – I think it was an Oracle system.
>
> **Leader** – Was it a MySQL database?
>
> **Judith** – I'm not sure.
>
> **Leader** – It's okay, I'm not that savvy with computers myself. I know enough to be dangerous. How did you get into the system?
>
> **Judith** – I could type in the customer's telephone number.
>
> **Leader** – That's the fastest way, only 10 keystrokes. You can also use the address, customer name or customer number.
>
> **Judith** – Sounds very similar.
>
> **Leader** – Good. You've had experience on a similar system, so this should be a breeze for you.
>
> **(Hands her step-by-step instructions)**
>
> **Leader** – Let's go over the process. First, you'll login to the system. Then open the database…
>
> **(The leader describes the process completely)**
>
> **Judith** – Seems pretty straight forward.

Understand the available information:

> **Leader** – Do you have any questions about the process?
>
> **Judith** – I don't think so.
>
> **Leader** – In that case, let me demonstrate.

Investigate alternatives:

(The leader sits at Judith's work station.)

Leader – When you get to work, you'll login, like this, with your personal ID and password. If you leave the building for lunch or at the end of the day, you'll need to logout.

Judith – Okay.

Leader – Let's say that Mrs. Wiley calls in to complain about her bill. At this screen, you can type in her phone number, which is 214-555-0977, hit the enter key, and voila! There is her account information. It's usually only two or three pages per account.

(The leader scrolls through the account and points out the various fields that might be needed.)

Judith – Got it.

Leader – Okay then, let's have you set up your ID and password.

(The leader logs out and then switches seats with Judith)

Leader – That is where you can create a password. Just click that button. Now, type in your ID, there.

Judith – Is my name ok?

Leader – Most people use their first initial and last name. Now, you can make up a password and verify it. Now, you're in. Let's logout and then log back in to make sure it's working.

Judith – Okay.

Leader – Good. Now, I will be Mr. Jones. Ring, Ring!

Judith – Hello, this is TGC, how may I help you?

Leader – This is Bob Jones. I just got an invoice for ten cases of Panatone latex paint, which I didn't order.

Judith – May I get your phone number Mr. Jones?

Leader – 972-555-3765.

Judith – Thank you, sir. I see an invoice amount of $1080. Is that the one you're talking about?

Leader – That's the one.

Judith – I'll remove that from your record. Have you received the paint?

Leader – Not yet.

Judith – Then I will send a note to shipping to make sure it doesn't go out. Is there anything else I can do for you today, Mr. Jones?

Leader – No, I appreciate you taking care of that so quickly.

Judith – My pleasure, you have a nice day. Good bye.

Leader – That was very good. I particularly liked that you were polite. You found the information quickly and verified what the customer was talking about and you offered to take the amount off the bill. The only upgrade I have for you is when you answered, you said, "Hello, this is TGC, how may I help you?" I'd like you to add two things: your name and department. So, it would sound like this, "Hello, you've reached TGC Customer Service my name is Judith. How may I help you?"

Judith – Okay, no problem.

Leader – Let's do another example. Ring, Ring!

(The leader should continue the practice session until satisfied that the new employee is performing the skill as expected)

Decide on the best course of action, Develop a plan, and Do it:

Leader – I'd say you are ready to go.

Judith – Sounds good.

Leader – I'll check back in about an hour to see how things are going and if you have any questions.

Judith – I'd appreciate that.

Leader – In the meantime, if you have any questions call me. If I'm not available, Brendan or Kelly are your best bet.

Judith – They've both been supportive so far.

Evaluate progress and results, Express gratitude:

Leader – That was a great practice session, Judith. I'm confident that you will represent the company well. See you in about an hour.

12

Developing Organizational Talent

---------------------------------- ⅄ ----------------------------------

INTRODUCTION

Developing Organizational Talent is one of the most important managerial responsibilities. This chapter covers the following behavioral competency:

Developing Organizational Talent – Planning the growth of employees so they can fulfill future responsibilities more effectively.

> ➢ Analyzing areas for development and setting specific goals
> ➢ Determining appropriate developmental activities
> ➢ Ensuring opportunities for development and removing obstacles
> ➢ Providing specific feedback

What is DOT?

DOT is the development of learned skills. In the domain of work, some general skills might include:

> ➢ Time management
> ➢ Teamwork
> ➢ Leadership
> ➢ Self-motivation

Why Do We DOT?

Developing Organizational Talent cultivates the learned capacity to carry out pre-determined results often with the minimum outlay of time, energy, or both.

How Do We DOT?

GUIDE is used to:

> ➢ Gather information about the competencies for the next level position
> ➢ Understand proficiency gaps in the employee
> ➢ Investigate alternatives for learning the required skills

> Decide on how to use the newly learned skills
> Evaluate use of the skills on the job

Behavioral Competencies for Leadership Levels:

Starting with Front Line Supervisor, consider how the five most important behavioral competencies might be different for these three positions:

Front Line Supervisor	Team Leader	Executive
Judgment	Judgment	Judgment
Individual Leadership	Group Leadership	Visionary Leadership
Tactical Planning	Project Planning	Strategic Planning
Tolerance for Stress	Internal Customer Orientation	Entrepreneurial Insight
Quantitative Analysis	Core Process Analysis	Organizational Systems Analysis

What is Developing Organizational Talent?

Helping people develop is one of your most important managerial responsibilities. Developing Organizational Talent is a process by which a supervisor evaluates the organization's future needs and compares those needs to the talent pool; then, plans development activities to build those competencies in individuals. Each individual plan should be based upon the employee's career ambition, personal interests, and learning style.

The Process:

Step 1 – Diagnose the development needs
Step 2 – Jointly prepare a plan for personal growth
Step 3 – Provide opportunities to apply newly learned skills on the job
Step 4 – Foster a learning environment and remove barriers to development

Diagnose the Development Needs

The diagnosis requires information. Some of the ways a supervisor can obtain the necessary information include:

> The annual performance appraisal
> 360° feedback survey
> Formal assessment centers

Applying GUIDE to Developing Organizational Talent

Gather Information

Seek the desires of the employee. Ask questions like, "What are your career ambitions?" "Which positions in the company are of interest to you?"

Understand the Available Information

Summarize your understanding of the available information and ask, "Is that correct?"

Investigate Alternatives

If you don't know already, you'll want to find out what the person's learning style and preferences are, then explore a variety of options which include:

> ➢ Job assignments that allow the employee to learn the necessary skills
> ➢ Special projects the person has never worked on before
> ➢ Continuing Education workshops that address a deficiency
> ➢ Self-study options (books, videos, audio programs)

Decide on the Best Course of Action, Develop a Plan, and Do It

Agree on a schedule of activities with deadlines.

Evaluate Progress and Results, Express Gratitude

Express confidence in the employee's ability to follow through on the developmental opportunities and ultimately reach the desired position.

Provide Opportunities to Apply Newly Learned Skills On the Job

Once a development activity has been completed, it's your job to provide opportunities to use the new skill as a part of the work. For instance, if your employee took a class in how to delegate, you should coach the employee before the first delegation. You should also help the employee evaluate the result of the delegation and provide feedback to ensure continued growth and improvement.

Foster a Learning Environment and Remove Barriers to Development

Fostering a learning environment means encouraging others to pursue educational opportunities and expand their capacity to create greater results. This requires a mental framework of a nurturing partner.

Too frequently supervisors pay lip service to this concept but put learning on the "back burner" when deadlines are tight or "the numbers" aren't met. An important part of your job is to remove any barriers to the development of future managers and executives, including your own behavior.

Positive Model: Developing Organizational Talent

Developing Organizational Talent is the best way to ensure a prosperous organization. It creates a talent pool for the company's succession plan. Those who don't pay attention to the career needs of staff jeopardize losing their best asset. Here is a sample of what might happen during this type of discussion for an Assistant Property Manager.

Gather information:

Leader – Chris, the purpose of this meeting is to discuss your career goals. As you know, one of our company's core values is to promote from within. This requires that we be proactive in the development of our best and brightest so we can get them into the positions that serve the company and each employee mutually. With that in mind, I'm interested in what your career ambitions are?

Chris – Well, I certainly would like to be a Property Manager.

Leader – Is there any particular property that interests you?

Chris – Actually that one near Lake Travis called Hill Country Manor.

Leader – That's a beautiful property. I wouldn't mind moving down there myself.

Chris – It sure seems like a great place to live.

Leader – Let me go over the results of our 360° survey with you (hands Chris a summary of the feedback). This shows the list of forty competencies that were included in the survey. They are listed from the top in descending order. These top ten represent your greatest strengths and these bottom ten represent developmental needs. Does anything surprise you?

Chris – Impact was my next to worst? How can that be?

Leader – I'm not sure what each individual was thinking about when responding to the survey, but generally this means when people observe you they are evaluating you as a leader and manager, how you handle yourself under pressure, that kind of thing.

Chris – Do you think I don't make a good first impression?

Leader – I think you have a good sense of confidence. Like I said, I'm not sure what others were thinking. Why don't you call Harry when we're finished here and see what his impressions are? Then we'll have a better idea of the best way to overcome that concern.

Chris – Okay, I will.

Understand the available information:

> **Leader** – So, based upon the survey, your top three strengths are Collaboration, Analysis, and Innovation. Your bottom three are Follow-up, Impact, and Selection and Promotion Decision-Making. Right?
>
> **Chris** – That's what it says.
>
> **Leader** – Let's look at what can be done about these.

Investigate alternatives:

> **Leader** – First, how do you like to learn best?
>
> **Chris** – What do you mean?
>
> **Leader** – I'm a visual learner; so, I prefer going to a seminar or watching a video.
>
> **Chris** – I think I'm the same way.
>
> **Leader** – Do you like to read business books?
>
> **Chris** – I'm a slow reader and get bored with it after a while.
>
> **Leader** – So, we should look for workshops first and then when you return, I'll give you some job assignments to apply the learning. Okay?
>
> **Chris** – Sounds good.
>
> **Leader** – Let's look at the strengths first.
>
> **Chris** – I thought this was about developing the weaknesses?
>
> **Leader** – It's about both. By looking at Collaboration first and ensuring that you are a conscious competent, we will build on that strength and may find a way to overcome another area where there is a proficiency gap. See?
>
> **Chris** – I get it.
>
> **Leader** – So, for Collaboration, one option might be for you to join a cross-functional improvement team and practice your ability to contribute to the group effort.
>
> **(This continues until Chris has a clear idea of what to do and they have agreement)**
>
> **Leader** – Okay let's move on to Selection and Promotion Decision-Making. What would you suggest for that one?
>
> **Chris** – I think the best bet is a workshop, for sure.

Leader – I know of an excellent one at Collin College run by a brilliant Professor named Simonds.

Chris – I'll go online and look for the next scheduled class.

Leader – Okay, great.

(This continues until all competencies have been covered, usually limited to between four and six)

Decide on the best course of action, Develop a plan, and Do it:

Leader – Just to make sure we're on the same page, why don't you summarize for me what you plan to do?

Chris – First thing I'm going to do is call Harry to find out why Impact was so low. Then I'm going to call Charlie and see if I can get on a CIT that is just starting the process. Then, I'm going to go online and register for the next Selection seminar at Collin….

Leader – And you also mentioned that video called, The Art of Managing People.

Chris – That's right (Chris makes a note).

Leader – Anything else?

Chris – I think that ought to cover it for now.

Evaluate progress and results, Express gratitude:

Leader – It may seem like a lot, Chris, but it's the best way to prepare you for that Property Manager's position in Austin. I think you have a great plan and I'm confident that you'll do well with these activities. Let me know what you find out on your calls and when you have finished the Selection class, we'll schedule you to do some interviewing for our team.

Section Four

Directing Employees
Toward Success

13

Delegating

---- ⅄ ----

INTRODUCTION

Delegating is one of the most important managerial responsibilities. This chapter covers the following behavioral competency:

Delegating – The process of transferring a specific job, function, or task from you to another. Steps include:

- ➢ Sorting tasks to be delegated
- ➢ Naming the delegate
- ➢ Defining the task in specific, measurable terms
- ➢ Assigning the appropriate level of authority

What is Delegating?

The dictionary defines delegating this way:

1. to entrust to another (authority) 2. to appoint as one's representative 3. to assign responsibility or authority:

A good manager knows how to delegate.

Why Do We Delegate?

Delegating empowers a subordinate to make decisions. It is a shift of decision-making authority from one organizational level to a lower one.

How Do We Delegate?

1. Tell why the job is important
2. Define the results you want
3. Define authority
4. Agree on a deadline
5. Ask for feedback
6. Set up controls

Barriers to Delegating

Effective delegating takes time. One barrier is the unwillingness to take the time to do it right. This barrier manifests in the manager thinking, "I can do this job faster or better if I just do it myself."

Most supervisors are promoted from the ranks of the front-line workers because they were excellent workers. When they become supervisors, they may lack confidence or skill in doing the managerial functions or they may enjoy doing the operating activities. So, they don't delegate those tasks.

Similarly, the new supervisor may lack confidence in the subordinates' abilities. Since he fears they will make mistakes, he refuses to delegate meaningful work.

Furthermore, the supervisor may delegate but then micromanage the project. This leads to ineffective use of the leader's time.

Some supervisors want to be "liked" by the troops and may think, "If I give this job to Bob, the rest of the people will accuse me of favoritism." Or, he may fear that the folks will think he's piling on too much work and he'll be disliked.

Delegating Tactics

Delegating is the transfer of a specific job, function, or task from you to another. It requires determining three things:

1. Responsibility
2. Accountability
3. Authority

Responsibility pertains to the task or assignment to be delegated. The manager should differentiate tasks by asking, "What tasks am I doing that…"

- ➤ Need not be done at all
- ➤ Could be done by someone else
- ➤ Only I must do

Accountability requires the manager to determine the specific guidelines for the assignment and to describe the obligation in terms of:

- ➤ Quality (acceptable number of errors permitted or rework)
- ➤ Quantity (number of products or services produced)
- ➤ Timeliness (milestones or deadlines)
- ➤ Cost (budget)

Most importantly, delegating also involves deciding upon a level of decision-making authority based upon the employee's maturity level. You know the person's level of willingness and ability, so select the authority most appropriate for the situation.

At maturity level one, the delegate is a beginner in the job and not feeling confident or competent. The supervisor should use a telling style and describe what to do, how to do it, and when. Say something like, "Do it exactly this way...." If the delegation is more of a project or problem to be solved, you might say, "Look into this problem and analyze the cause; then we'll decide together."

Maturity level two means the delegate has gained some success, willingness to take on the responsibility has increased, but ability may still be low; so, the boss should use a coaching style to influence the decisions. Say something like, "Describe the circumstances and what you need from me to assess and handle it." Then coach the employee through the decision. To help the employee move closer to the next level, use GUIDE to explore the root causes, options for solving the problem, pros and cons of each, and the final recommendation. Use SPIN to provide reinforcing or corrective feedback as you go through the GUIDE process.

When a person is clearly at maturity level three, the effective leader should use a consulting style to increase the employee's willingness to assume responsibility. You might say something like, "Decide and take action. There is no need to discuss it with me unless you need my help. Let me know what you did and the results in your monthly report."

Finally, a coordinator style is used when the employee is performing at a high achiever level four. The leader may simply state the objectives of the task and allow the employee to figure out how, when, and what is necessary. Say, "Decide and manage the situation, it's officially your area of responsibility now."

The Process

Step 1 – Sort through your tasks for work that should be delegated.

Step 2 – Select the delegate. The selection should be based upon each person's ability, experience, and confidence. Choose a person for which this assignment will be an upgrade in responsibility, a stimulating challenge, or a prerequisite for promotion.

Step 3 – Prepare for the briefing. Use a Discussion GUIDE form. Make notes of the information you want to give and the questions you might ask. Determine how you will involve the employee in investigating alternatives. Set appropriate follow-up dates for monitoring progress or coaching. Also, make notes of any opportunities to use CARE.

Step 4 – Schedule and conduct the face-to-face meeting.

Applying GUIDE to Delegating

Gather Information

In this discussion, most of the information gathered will be about the experiences the employee may have had with any similar types of jobs. Ask questions like, "Tell me about a time when you have done something like this?" "Have you ever been responsible for _____?"

Understand the Available Information

Here you might want to summarize your understanding of the employee's attitudes, skills, and knowledge (A.S.K.) in this area of responsibility and then say, "Did I miss anything?"

Investigate Alternatives

This is where you will describe the responsibly, accountability, and authority you intend to delegate. You should involve the employee in accordance with the maturity level as described earlier in this chapter.

Decide on the Best Course of Action, **D**evelop a Plan, and **D**o It

Seek the employee's commitment to taking on the task and a summary of perceived agreements. Assuming the employee's summary is accurate, you might end this step by asking, "Do you need anything else from me at this time?"

Evaluate Progress and Results, **E**xpress Gratitude

Set a follow-up date and conclude by expressing confidence in the employee's ability to complete the task successfully.

Positive Model: Delegating

Delegating is not dumping your undesirable tasks on an unsuspecting employee. Effective delegation requires an examination of all the tasks under your area of responsibility and comparing them to the A.S.K. of the employees available to do the work. Done correctly, delegating can expand the results you can achieve and develop your organization's talent. Here is a sample of what might happen during this type of discussion for a Training Manager.

Gather information:

> **Leader** – Betty, have a seat. I'd like to talk to you about a new responsibility I'd like you to assume. In the past, I've done all the scheduling of workshops, both public and in-house. I think it's time for you to take on a bit more responsibility and get the recognition you deserve. So, the purpose of this meeting is to discuss job responsibilities and answer any questions you might have about accepting it. Why don't you tell me about any experiences you've had with respect to scheduling.
>
> **Betty** – Well, it's somewhat limited. I've always been an individual contributor; so, naturally, I've had to schedule my own workshop, make sure the training room was available, all the materials were ordered, and the logistics were coordinated with the administrative staff... that kind of thing.
>
> **Leader** – Have you ever been responsible for other trainers, booked rooms for other speakers, or executives?
>
> **Betty** – Well, now that you mention it. I helped coordinate a presentation Tom Peters made at our company. And, in my last job, I was the liaison for two extra consultants. One taught two subjects, time management and stress management, and the other taught a teamwork class... Come to think of it, I also worked with two consultants in my first position.

Understand the available information:

> **Leader** – Good, so you know how to schedule the training rooms, work with support staff to make sure materials are prepared and arrive on schedule, right?
>
> **Betty** – That's right.

Investigate alternatives:

> **Leader** – Great. Let's explore the areas of this responsibility and see how you're feeling about it?

Betty – All right.

Leader – First, you'll be putting together the public workshop schedule and be accountable for ample coverage of all four of our product lines spread throughout the year. Any ideas on how you would handle that?

Betty – It's my understanding that the Supervisory Skills Certificate Program represents about half of our revenue. Then Selection Interviewing, IPM, and Executive Leadership stair-step down from that. Right?

Leader – That's right.

Betty – If we offered twenty-six workshops per year, half could be Supervisory Skills with the others presented in proportion to the revenue they generate. I could alternate them so there's never two of the same in a row.

Leader – Excellent strategy. It provides ample coverage with room to add other things as they come up, especially if you schedule them every other week. I like your thinking. You'll also be scheduling the trainers, both for the public workshops and in-house workshops, as well as the direct delivery workshops. What are your thoughts about that?

Betty – The in-house certifications and direct delivery workshops can't be planned in advance. They are dependent upon the account executives selling the programs. As you mentioned, I could alternate the public dates so only two workshops are scheduled in any one month, which leaves two weeks per month for the other types of workshops.

Leader – What about the trainers?

Betty – Geri is qualified for Soup skills and SIC. Mark can do Soup skills and IPM. I'm the only one qualified for ELC. Maybe I should build a matrix and slot all the workshops and trainers into it.

Leader – Any contingencies?

Betty – Well, we have six stringers, right?

Leader – Seven actually. I'll contact them to let them know you're taking over this responsibility. Do you have any other ideas or questions?

Betty – What is my decision-making authority?

Leader – I was thinking, for this first attempt, you might want to give me your analysis of the situation, put together your recommendations, and then we can talk about it and decide together.

(This continues until they have completed discussing all related issues)

Decide on the best course of action, Develop a plan, and Do it:

> **Leader** – Okay, Betty, does this sound like something you'd be interested in taking on?
>
> **Betty** – Absolutely.
>
> **Leader** – Then, based upon what we've discussed, why don't you summarize for me what you plan to do for scheduling next year's workshops?
>
> **Betty** – First, I'll put together a matrix including proposed workshops and locations, then assign trainers to each. I will review the plan with you. If you approve, I will distribute it to all the territory offices and inform corporate of our plans.
>
> **Leader** – That sounds great. I'm excited that you're going to take on this important responsibility. Is there anything else you need from me?
>
> **Betty** – I don't think so. I appreciate the opportunity.

Evaluate progress and results, Express gratitude:

> **Leader** – All right, I think we have agreement on a plan. Thank you for your help on this, Betty. I'm confident that you are the right person for this job. When should we meet again?
>
> **Betty** – Are you available next Wednesday?
>
> **Leader** – How's 9:00 AM for you?
>
> **Betty** – Perfect.
>
> **Leader** – I'll see you then.

14

Inspiring Desired Actions

INTRODUCTION

Inspiring someone as a counselor, teacher, coach, or mentor is one of the most important uses of the GUIDE process. Indeed, it was the first module written and delivered as a public workshop. The term "coaching" is used because of the analogies that can be drawn to managing or supervising others. This chapter covers the following behavioral competency:

Inspiring Desired Actions – Providing timely guidance and feedback to accomplish a task or solve a problem by:

> ➢ Clarifying expected behavior and level of proficiency
> ➢ Providing instruction, positive models, or seeking suggestions for improvement
> ➢ Establishing opportunities for observation
> ➢ Reinforcing successes or offering corrective feedback

What Is Coaching?

The dictionary defines coaching this way:

to give instruction or advice to in the capacity of a coach; instruct:

She has coached the present tennis champion.

Why Do We Coach?

The purpose of coaching is to identify the skills and capabilities that are within individuals, enabling them to use those skills and capabilities to the best of their ability.

How Do We Coach?

1. Document the need
2. Discuss methods for improvement
3. Determine when to observe

4. Watch for effective and ineffective behavior
5. Give immediate feedback

COACHING TACTICS

Coaching is a discussion between you and your employee in which there is a need to help the employee by providing timely guidance and feedback to accomplish a task or solve a problem.

Examples of coaching conversations include:

➢ Improving an employee's below-standard performance
➢ Improving work habits like absenteeism, tardiness, initiative, etc.
➢ Increasing assertiveness or decreasing aggressiveness
➢ Enhancing a skill like public speaking or meeting leadership
➢ Providing a fair warning of pending discipline
➢ Utilizing discipline effectively
➢ Improving professionalism in appearance or business decorum
➢ Increasing consideration of others in diverse work groups
➢ Assisting someone with personal problems that are effecting his work

The chart below shows a progression of steps that should be followed when attempting to correct a performance problem. The EEOC has specific requirements that must be met to ensure fair treatment of employees who may be fired for cause.

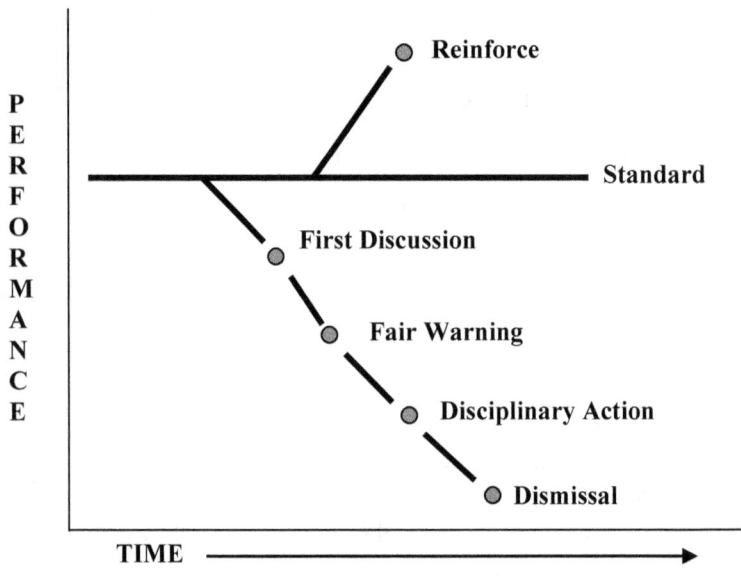

The First Discussion – This is the first time the employee is made aware that you have a problem with this person's performance. The meeting should follow the GUIDE process. Your demeanor in this meeting should be positive. While you may be concerned, even frustrated that the employee is not performing well, it's important for your attitude to be positive. Go into the meeting thinking, *with my help this employee will correct this issue.*

Fair Warning – This meeting is a follow-up to the First Discussion. If the person has not improved or performance is worse, you will conduct a second discussion very much like the first one, with one exception. Just before moving out of the D into the E of GUIDE, you'll want to say these words, "It's only fair to warn you that if this doesn't resolve the issue, the next step will be disciplinary action." You'll also want to add what the discipline will be. This is based upon your company's policies; such as, "a three-day suspension without pay." Check with a Human Resources Representative or your policy manual to make sure you have the correct disciplinary action. Finally, you should be prepared for a defensive or emotional reaction. If you get one, say something like, "This isn't something I want to do and if you do what we just agreed to, the problem will be corrected and I won't have to go further." Then move to the closing step and express confidence in the employee's ability to correct the problem.

Disciplinary Action – This is the follow-up meeting to the Fair Warning meeting. If the problem remains the same or gets worse, you'll have to execute the discipline. You'll simply say, "The last time we talked, I said, 'If the problem were not resolved, I'd have to issue disciplinary leave.' Unfortunately, that will have to happen today. I want to see you in three days' time, when you arrive to work." When the person returns in three days, you will conduct a GUIDE meeting in the usual fashion until you get to the end of the D. At that point you need to say these words, "I think we have a plan that will work. If it doesn't the next step will be dismissal." Once again, you'll need to be ready for Empathy and to reassure the employee that success is highly probable. Finally, you'll want to document this one in a memo to the employee with copies to your boss and the personnel department.

Dismissal – If the employee does not correct the problem after three GUIDE meetings, it is unlikely that it will be corrected and you may fire the employee. The EEOC requires three attempts as a minimum. You may offer more chances, but assuming you used GUIDE and CARE and the meetings ended on a positive note, you have met the EEOC criteria.

Reinforce – If you use GUIDE and CARE as described, you have an 80% chance of success during any of the aforementioned meetings. Let's say over the course of your career, you have to speak to one hundred individuals who have performance or work habits problems. During the First Discussion eighty of them will respond favorably to the GUIDE meeting and improve. Twenty will go to the Fair Warning stage and sixteen of those will improve. Four will go to the Disciplinary stage and three of those will improve. By probability, you will have to fire only one person in one hundred during your career.

At any point during the cycle of these meetings, should the person's performance get back to or exceed expectations, you should conduct the reinforcing meeting. The meeting shouldn't last longer than five minutes emphasizing the G, U, and E of the GUIDE process as well as the R of CARE. This meeting should be 100% positive. Don't try to get more from the employee. Just praise the accomplishment and end the meeting.

The Process:

Step 1 – Determine the need for coaching by observing the employee's behavior.

Step 2 – Prepare for the meeting. Use a Discussion GUIDE form. Make notes of the information you want to give and the questions you might ask. Determine how you will involve the employee in investigating alternatives. Set appropriate follow-up dates for monitoring progress or providing feedback. Also, plan for opportunities to use CARE.

Step 3 – Schedule and conduct the face to face meeting.

Step 4 – Arrange for practice, if appropriate. Observe and provide feedback.

Applying GUIDE to Coaching

Gather Information

More often than not, this discussion is about a problem with performance or work habits not meeting expectations. Ultimately, you need to know why performance has fallen below standard without sounding like a nagging parent. Ask questions like, "What's causing this?" "When did this start happening?"

Understand the Available Information

Summarize your understanding of the causes of the problem. Then say, "Is that right?" or "Is there anything else?" before moving on.

Investigate Alternatives

Seek ideas for solving the problem. If the employee cannot or will not participate, be patient. Try to avoid issuing orders. The employee will be motivated to change, if the ideas are his.

Decide on the Best Course of Action, Develop a Plan, and Do It

Seek the employee's commitment to take corrective action and a summary of perceived agreements. Compare the employee's summary to your own understanding.

Evaluate Progress and Results, Express Gratitude

Set a follow-up date and conclude by expressing confidence in the employee's ability to correct the problem by following the agreed upon plan.

Positive Model: Coaching

You will need to address work habits issues like absenteeism, tardiness, initiative, etc. soon. If you are silent too long the employee may assume the behavior is acceptable. Here is a sample of what might happen during this type of discussion with an Administrative Assistant.

Gather information:

> **Leader** – Pam, the purpose of this meeting is to review your attendance (hands her the attendance report). Lately, I've noticed that it has been difficult for you to get to work on time. I wanted us to put our heads together and figure out how to stop this pattern before it really starts affecting your record.
>
> **Pam** – There's no pattern!
>
> **Leader** – As you can see, the record shows you've been tardy three days this week and five days last week.
>
> **Pam** – Yeah, but there's no pattern. I have a different excuse for each time.
>
> **Leader** – Pam, this morning Ed asked me for the Exxon project report. You weren't here and I looked everywhere for it. Not having that report when he asked me makes this department look bad. It reflects poorly on Ann, on me, and on you. I need you here, on time, working at 7:30; so, we must find a solution to this problem. Tell me about the causes?
>
> **Pam** – Well, today there was a train stuck on the railroad track for a good fifteen minutes.
>
> **Leader** – I know how much anxiety that can cause. You're stuck, can't move, and feel there is nothing you can do about it.
>
> **Pam** – Right.
>
> **Leader** – What about yesterday?
>
> **Pam** – Yesterday, my daughter woke late and I had to take her to school, which is in the other direction. Monday, my Mother fell and I couldn't just leave her on the floor. Etcetera, etcetera, etcetera.
>
> **Leader** – Anything else?
>
> **Pam** – No, that's all.
>
> **Leader** – Okay.

Understand the available information:

> **Leader** – So, you have been tardy between three and five days per week for the last three weeks. Apparently, there have been a variety of reasons for this. You feel these are all out of your control. Is that right?
>
> **Pam** – Right.

Investigate alternatives:

> **Leader** – Pam, I wouldn't expect you to be tardy more than three to five days every year. I think it is a serious issue…given what we've just talked about, what ideas do you have for correcting the problem?
>
> **Pam** – I guess you could give me a wake-up call.
>
> **Leader** – Well, I can't do that, but I can help you think through other alternatives. Do you think it is just a matter of getting up earlier?
>
> **Pam** – Probably.
>
> **Leader** – Then what alternatives, besides me calling, are available to you?
>
> **Pam** – My husband and daughter are very dependent on me in the mornings. I could have a talk with them and ask for their help.
>
> **Leader** – That's a wise first step, anything else?
>
> **Pam** – I guess we could see what they say and then consider other possibilities.
>
> **Leader** – I'd rather we explore all the possibilities now.
>
> **Pam** – I could set my alarm fifteen to twenty minutes earlier.
>
> **Leader** – That makes sense. What about a contingency for the alarm?
>
> **Pam** – What do you mean?
>
> **Leader** – You said you wanted a wake-up call, they have services for that or, perhaps a second alarm clock.
>
> **Pam** – I could check into that.
>
> **Leader** – Good, any other ideas?
>
> **(This continues until they have completed the brainstorming)**

Decide on the best course of action, Develop a plan, and Do it:

> **Leader** – Okay, Pam, based upon what we've discussed, why don't you summarize for me what you plan to do?

Pam – First, I will talk to my family members and let them know I need their support. I will buy a second alarm clock and set it on the dresser so I have to get out of bed to turn it off.

Leader – When?

Pam – Tonight.

Leader – Great. Let's meet again in one week at the same time to check progress.

Pam – Okay.

Evaluate progress and results, Express gratitude:

Leader – Great, I think this plan will work for you. As I said earlier, you are an important part of our team. I appreciate your commitment to being here during scheduled business hours. Thank you for your help on this, Pam.

Pam – You're welcome.

Leader – In the meantime, feel free to come to me with any other issues you may have.

Positive Model: Reinforcing

Specific and sincere reinforcement means honest feedback that encourages a person to continue the desired behavior. Here is a sample of what might happen if the aforementioned Administrative Assistant corrected the tardiness problem.

Gather information:

> **Leader** – Pam, over the past week, I've notice you've been at your desk working at 7:30 every day. Thanks, I appreciate the effort.
>
> **Pam** – No problem.
>
> **Leader** – What seemed to help the most?
>
> **Pam** – I followed our plan. My family didn't realize they were interfering with my getting to work. With the second alarm, I'm not likely to hit snooze and get back in bed.

Understand the available information:

> **Leader** – Well apparently your ideas worked well. I also heard from Ed. He said because you were here early yesterday, he was able to get information he needed for the Executive Committee meeting.
>
> **Pam** – Glad I could help.

Investigate alternatives:

Decide on the best course of action, Develop a plan, and Do it:

Evaluate progress and results, Express gratitude:

> **Leader** – I'm pleased with the way you handled the situation, congratulations. Also, by being on time it helps us both be more productive and less stressed. Thanks Pam, I value the discipline.

15

Coordinating Team Efforts

———————————— ⅄ ————————————

INTRODUCTION

Coordinating Team Efforts is important in situations where you are involved in a task force, executive committee, or a self-directed work team. This chapter covers the following behavioral competency:

Coordinating Team Efforts – Using appropriate and flexible styles to build cohesive work groups. The key actions should include:

➢ Guiding the development of purpose, goals and objectives
➢ Clarifying the roles and responsibilities of team members
➢ Providing necessary resources and removing obstacles to team success
➢ Utilizing individual differences and talents
➢ Demonstrating personal commitment to the team

What is a Team?

The dictionary defines team this way:

a number of persons associated in some joint action:

A team of advisers.

Types of Teams

The most obvious types of teams are:

➢ Problem-Solving Teams – Temporary task forces or Action Research teams that are formed to resolve a specific problem and then disbanded
➢ Self-Directed Work Teams – Groups of employees with no formal supervisor who produce products or services and make their own business decisions
➢ Leadership Teams – The executive team of CEO and the direct reports

Teambuilding Stages:

1. Forming – The honeymoon stage where team members get to know each other
2. Storming – When differing views cause conflict and rivalry for leadership
3. Norming – When the team develops a charter with ground rules, purpose, etc.
4. Performing – When the team starts to reach its goals and achieve results

TACTICS FOR COORDINATING TEAM EFFORTS

A team is not just a group of people who work together in the same department. To be a team, the individuals must spend their energy focused on reaching organizational goals. It holds that one of the most important tactics then is to have a clear *sense of direction*. Assuming you are the team leader, you will want to hold a meeting to agree on the team's purpose and specific goals. The outcome of the meeting should be commitment to group decisions, deadlines, and results.

Another important component to team success is *accountability*. As has been publicized, members of sports teams hold each other accountable. If a teammate breaks a rule or slacks off, the manager or head coach often expects a veteran player to pull his mate aside and set him straight. As the team leader, you should encourage that practice.

Finally, *trust* is a crucial element of team excellence. Without trust, team members are likely to hide mistakes or blame others, make assumptions about other's intentions, hold grudges, etc. You can build trust by creating an environment that does not punish people for making mistakes and encourages openness. The best way to build trust on teams is to:

> ➤ Practice CARE within the team – Stand up for one another. Praise each other when appropriate. Listen and respond with Empathy. Avoid criticism, use SPIN instead.

> ➤ Keep sensitive information confidential – Honor the other team members by avoiding gossip or disclosing private or classified sentiments.

> ➤ Appreciate differences in styles, abilities, and motivations – Don't focus on racial diversity. Considering differences in personality, skills, and desires results in team success.

The Process:

> Step 1 – Select members for the team
> Step 2 – Develop team's purpose and principles
> Step 3 – Develop meeting ground rules and procedures
> Step 4 – Identify team's customers, products, and services
> Step 5 – Define roles and responsibilities
> Step 6 – Identify the team's business measures (SMART goals, accountability, etc.)
> Step 7 – Take action to accomplish the team's purpose
> Step 8 – Reward and Reboot, or Disband

Applying GUIDE to Teams

Essentially, GUIDE is used exactly the same way with groups of people as it is with individuals. Let's assume you are going to facilitate a meeting with your newly formed team to develop its charter. You would:

*G*ather Information

Have team members introduce themselves and seek information about the members' past experience on teams. Ask questions like, "Have you ever worked on a cross-functional team?" "How would you describe the experience?" "What were the results?"

Also, ask questions about the gap you are trying to close, such as, "What is the problem or project we will be working on?" "Why are we together?" "Why is this project worth doing?" "Why now?" "Who owns the problem?" "What are the consequences of not doing this project?" "What will be different once we've finished working together?"

*U*nderstand the Available Information

Summarize your understanding of the purpose and importance of the team and the direction the team intends to go. Then, because this is a group of four to six people, make eye contact with each one and check for agreement. Say, "Is that how you see it?" or "Do you have any doubt?" If all agree, move on.

*I*nvestigate Alternatives

Seek ideas for completing the charter document. The items to be covered and agreed upon are Ground Rules, Tasks, Constraints, How meetings will be run, Roles and Responsibilities, Project Scope, Expected Deliverables, Budget, and Documentation.

I would suggest looping from Investigate to Decide on each individual item, then back to Investigate for the second item, and so on until you have completed all items.

Decide on the Best Course of Action, **D**evelop a Plan, and **D**o It

After the team has agreed to all the items, let the group know you will have the charter typed and delivered to each team member for review. Ask them to evaluate it and make notes about possible revisions.

Evaluate Progress and Results, **E**xpress Gratitude

Set a follow-up date to revisit the typed charter. Thank the committee members for their commitment to working on the project.

Team Charter Agenda

Desired Outcomes

By the end of this meeting we will have:

- ➤ Reviewed critical elements of the charter
- ➤ Generated a list of alternative courses of action
- ➤ Agreed upon the charter document

Ground Rules

1. Seek consensus
2. Be positive and respectful
3. Listen with full attention
4. Honor time commitments
5. Emergency notification

Choice of Decision-Making Method

Consensus with a fallback to use weighted voting

GUIDE	Process Steps	Lead	Time
Start-up	Step 1 - Member introductions - Select a time keeper - Review desired outcomes, agenda, decision-making options and ground rules	All	2:00 PM 5'
Gather information Understand the available information	Step 2 - Seek brief history - Check for understanding & agreement	All	2:05 5'
Investigate alternatives	Step 3 - Develop a list of preliminary ideas for Ground Rules, Tasks, Constraints, How meetings will be run, Roles and Responsibilities, Project Scope, Expected Deliverables, Budget, and Documentation - Clarify - Combine or Eliminate	Team Lead Facilitates All members participate	2:10 40'
Decide on the best course of action, Develop a plan, and Do it	Step 4 - Summarize agreements	All	2:50 5'
Evaluate the meeting	Step 5 +/Δ Evaluation	All	2:55 5'
		Total	3:00 60'

16

Resolving Conflict

———————— 人 ————————

INTRODUCTION

Resolving Conflict is one of my most requested sessions. This chapter covers the following behavioral competency:

Resolving Conflict – Using appropriate and flexible styles to reduce tension in antagonistic situations between two or more people.

> ➢ Gathering information to understand the conflict
> ➢ Considering both sides of the issue
> ➢ Avoiding personal attacks
> ➢ Seeking alternative positive courses of action
> ➢ Mediating to maintain relationships
> ➢ Summarizing agreements and required actions

What Is a Conflict?

The dictionary defines conflict this way:

1. to come into collision or disagreement 2. be contradictory, at variance 3. in opposition or to clash 4. to fight or contend 5. do battle:

The account of one eyewitness
conflicted with that of the other.

Why Do We Resolve Conflict?

The purpose of resolving conflict is to reduce a perceived threat to the involved parties' needs, interests, or concerns, and to discover new opportunities, especially when working in teams.

How Do We Resolve Conflict?

Through one of various negotiating tactics, such as:

> ➢ Competing
> ➢ Accommodating
> ➢ Avoiding
> ➢ Compromising
> ➢ Collaborating

TACTICS FOR RESOLVING CONFLICT

Competing is typically used when I perceive my needs are more important than yours. This leads to a win-lose outcome in which I win and you lose. People may prefer to compete because they have been taught to be competitive when dealing with others or perhaps they just enjoy it. In business, I regress to competing only when the other party refuses to negotiate in good faith.

Accommodating means I feel that your needs are more important than mine. Using this tactic results in a lose-win outcome in which I lose and you win. In many family situations you may find it is the easiest way to reach a peaceful outcome. Taking the path of least resistance is not usually recommended with your employees.

Avoiding means no one is talking about needs. This yields a lose-lose outcome, so both parties lose. This tactic is dysfunctional in most any context. It is contrary to CAREing for your employees.

Compromising is like bargaining. In Mexican border towns, the merchants actually expect Americans to engage them in a back and forth banter to reach agreement on a price. It's not what I call effective negotiating and can be less satisfying, lead to unwise decisions, low trust, and endanger relationships. In many cases, it leads to revenge syndrome which means the next time we get together, I'll get even.

Collaborating is true negotiating where the parties pool their needs and goals toward a common purpose. This results in a win-win outcome where both sides win. It develops mutual trust which frees the parties to discuss the issues openly.

The Process:

Conflicts contain substantive, procedural, and psychological dimensions that need to be negotiated.

> Step 1 - Separate Task and Relationships (GUIDE and CARE)
> Step 2 - Avoid Taking a Stand (listen with full attention)

Step 3 - Be Creative (explore all the options)
Step 4 - Develop Objective Criteria (how will the decision be made)

Applying GUIDE to Resolving Conflict

The conflict could be between you and another employee or it could be between two other employees that requires you to intervene.

*G*ather Information

Your goal is to understand why the other person is upset. Seek information about what has happened to cause the conflict. Using a friendly tone, ask, "What's going on?" "You seem angry, why?" "Tell me about your concerns?"

Use of the CARE behaviors, especially Empathy, will be critical to success. At the beginning, tempers may be running hot. You'll need to get the people past the interfering emotions before getting into the substance of the conflict.

*U*nderstand the Available Information

Summarize your understanding of the perceived threat to the employee's needs, interest, or concerns. Then, say, "Is that how you see it?"

*I*nvestigate Alternatives

Seek ideas for correcting the substance of the issue or changing the perception. In most cases the conflict is based upon fear. Without accusing the person of being fearful, seek ideas about what will relieve the fear. Ask, "What do you think we could do to resolve the issue?"

If this is between two other employees, ask, "How can we resolve this to the satisfaction of both your needs?"

*D*ecide on the best course of action, *D*evelop a plan, and *D*o it

Ask the employees to summarize the negotiated agreement. You might simply ask, "What do you plan to do next?"

*E*valuate progress and results, *E*xpress gratitude

Set a follow-up date if you feel it's necessary. Thank the employees for their collaboration on the issue.

Positive Model: Resolving Conflict

The need to resolve conflict doesn't happen often, but when it does, utilizing effective negotiating behavior will help most. If you focus on the employees' interests rather than positions, you'll be able to invent options for mutual gain. Here is a sample of what might happen during this type of discussion for a Production Manager.

Gather information:

> **Leader** – Steve, the purpose of this meeting is to review progress toward our team's objective of cross-training all the machine operators. Recently, some of the other operators have told me that you aren't training them as scheduled. What's going on?
>
> **Steve** – I'm not sure cross-training is critical to continuous improvement.
>
> **Leader** – I thought you were supportive of the team's decision?
>
> **Steve** – I was, but I've had second thoughts.
>
> **Leader** – Tell me about your thoughts?
>
> **Steve** – I'm the only person to master the operation of the clarifier machine. It's not fair to ask me to give that up and it won't help with continuous improvement to allow someone less competent to work that machine.
>
> **Leader** – You sound upset. Are you afraid that training others will lessen your value or threaten your job security?
>
> **Steve** – Yes, you could say that.
>
> **Leader** – Is there anything else that bothers you?
>
> **Steve** – Rotating jobs may be good for the new guys, but asking me to run those machines is a slap in the face.
>
> **Leader** – You feel you've graduated from working on those simple machines. Is that it?
>
> **Steve** – Exactly.
>
> **Leader** – Are there any other problems?
>
> **Steve** – No, that's it.
>
> **Leader** – Okay, let me recap....

Understand the available information:

> **Leader** – You feel training others is a threat to your seniority and working the simpler machines is an insult based upon your skills and experience. Is that right?

Steve – Right.

Investigate alternatives:

> **Leader** – Steve, I can assure you that cross-training is not a threat to your seniority…you've been with us for nine years and I consider you the most experienced machine operator in the company. Also, I need your leadership on this team…with that in mind, what ideas do you have for increasing the other's skill and confidence?

> **Steve** – I don't know.

> **Leader** – Well what helped you, when you were learning? How did you gain the skills and experience to get where you are today?

> **Steve** – Before Bill retired he taught me some short cuts.

> **Leader** – Wouldn't it be possible for you to do the same with some of the new guys?

> **Steve** – I suppose so, but can you guarantee I won't lose my machine?

> **Leader** – Yes. Letting someone else learn your machine would only be used if you were out sick. Also, I have a theory that you can't get promoted unless there is someone competent to take over your work.

> **Steve** – Well, that makes sense.

> **Leader** – I can understand why you might feel awkward training someone on your turf. The team did decide to use cross-training to meet our continuous improvement goals. Can you help us achieve our cross-training goal?

> **Steve** – I care very much about the good of the team.

> **Leader** – I know you do. Are there any other ways to accomplish our goal?

> **Steve** – No, I guess not.

> **(This continues until the idea pool is exhausted)**

Decide on the best course of action, Develop a plan, and Do it:

> **Leader** – Okay, Steve, based upon what we've discussed, why don't you summarize for me what you plan to do next?

> **Steve** – Tomorrow, I'll ask James to spend some time with me on the clarifying machine. Together we'll put together a schedule to make sure he's feeling confident on this machine in the shortest period.

> **Leader** – That sounds great. I think James is an excellent choice as your first trainee. Is there anything else you need from me?

Steve – I don't think so. Thanks for your reassurance.

Evaluate progress and results, Express gratitude:

> **Leader** – Thank you for your help on this, Steve. I'm confident that if you follow the plan we outlined today, you will be able to help the team reach its continuous improvement goals. Why don't you let me know how your first session goes with James?
>
> **Steve** – Okay, no problem.
>
> **Leader** – See you tomorrow.

Section Five

Change
at Work

17

System Theory

———————————— ⋏ ————————————

INTRODUCTION

Managing Change at Work is essential to the success of the organization. The next four chapters will cover the following behavioral competency:

Managing Change – The process of encouraging the imagination so employees will innovate new products or improve processes to add value to the customer. Knowledge areas include:

- ➢ System Theory
- ➢ Psychology of Habits and Attitudes
- ➢ Techniques of Group Process
- ➢ Creative Thinking Methodology
- ➢ Project Management

Organizations must embrace continuous improvement, question conventional wisdom, and promote change at work. Periodically reinventing the organization or product base will create the competitive advantage a company needs to profit and prosper in the future. Yet many people claim they don't like change. Overcoming resistance to change has been a hot topic for years, but may be somewhat misunderstood.

In *Organizing Change*, Lee and Krayer suggest four basic reasons why people resist change. They are:

1. Lack of involvement in the process;
2. Lack of knowledge about the change;
3. Insecurity about the future as a result of the change; and
4. Feelings of powerlessness to control their own destinies.

The question is what can be done to affect an organization to include change in day-to-day management and avoid the resistance? First, rename it "innovation." Innovation means the generation of ideas that bring about change.

People need to be able to tap creativity at will but unfortunately have been trained to suppress their creative powers. They need to be able to systematically make greater use of their potential. Furthermore, managers in organizations need to be able to build the management of innovation into their daily routines.

Individuals are naturally creative, active information processors, which mean our brains naturally change things, add to things, and create things. One dilemma is how we define what is truly creative. There is a range of creativity from adaptive to artistically creative. What is called creative is in the mind of the beholder.

Basically, each person has a threshold of acceptability related to ideas. For instance, some people say that Alexander Graham Bell was not creative when he invented the telephone. However, he was innovative. He invented something that changed our lives. Innovation is the process of change and implies that if a thing has changed enough, it was a creative idea that caused that change. Bell's telephone may not have been artistically creative in the sense that he did not develop a previously non-existent item. He was inspired by the telegraph, but he adapted, added to and changed the existing technology. That's what's called innovation.

This section is based upon five critical skills and knowledge areas that have been proven to be successful in a variety of settings. They are:

> System Theory
> Psychology of Habits and Attitudes
> Techniques of Group Process
> Creative Thinking Methodology
> Project Management

These five components will be discussed in detail in the chapters that follow and can be utilized in at least five major categories, and they are:

> A Continuous Improvement Intervention
> A Creative Problem Solving Method
> An Innovation Management System
> A Source of Business Profits
> A Reengineering Process

In this section, participants will *learn to think differently* about what they do and how they are doing it. They will learn how to initiate change that will drive the organization's growth because they will understand the importance of profitable and efficient procedures in design, production, distribution and maintenance of products and services.

The best companies see innovation as a function that needs managing and then they manage it by basing new products on customer needs, encouraging employees to use the expertise of the whole company, giving workers incentives for successful innovation and refusing to punish those who gamble and it doesn't pay off.

The productivity of the company doesn't have to be left to chance. It can be controlled and improved by involving everyone in generating new ways of creating and keeping customers through simple and continuous process improvements. It can be done through Change at Work.

To put this section into perspective, let's look at the historical context. These concepts have been around and evolved through the centuries. The quality movement can trace its roots back to medieval Europe. Here are the highlights:

> Guilds 13th Century
> Fredrick W. Taylor (Taylor System) 1800's
> Walter Shewhart (SQC) 1920's
> W. Edwards Deming (Father of Quality) 1938
> Total Quality Movement late 1940's
> Joseph M. Juran (Quality Control Handbook) 1951
> Kaizen (Japanese for "Change for the better") 1950's
> Quality Circles 1961
> Synectics 1970
> Resources Management 1980
> Six Sigma (Motorola) 1986
> ISO – 9000 standards & Malcolm Baldrige 1987
> Innovation Process Management 1994
> Customer Value Management mid – 1990's

This Change at Work Model comes from analyzing and synthesizing the processes of various writers. A literature review of 137 articles and books was conducted and this positive model for managing a change effort is summarized in these five steps:

Steps to Increase the Probability of Success:

1. Organize the Effort
2. Evaluate
3. Invent
4. Synthesize
5. Plan the Implementation

Organize the Effort – involves:

> Forming Action Research Teams (ART), including selecting team members and defining roles and responsibilities;
> Establishing infrastructures;
> Securing management support; and
> Establishing systems for planning, information flow, and customer feedback.

Evaluate – includes:

> Establishing a purpose (vision, mission, goals);
> Defining the need for change (the gap) either through problem identification, defining a higher performance goal, or describing an opportunity for a new product or service;
> Providing a history of the problem or opportunity through qualitative or quantitative data;
> Developing an "As Is" process map; and
> Ensuring understanding of ART members' outputs.

Invent – means:

> Recognizing the creativity of people;
> Increasing synergistic teamwork by reducing inhibitive behaviors;
> Generating large numbers of ideas; and
> Creating distance from the problem and encouraging non-rational thinking.

Synthesize – involves:

> Forcing the imaginative ideas into logical, rational conclusions;
> Combining components into a complete solution;
> Recognizing the importance of a critical evaluator;
> Deciding what should be done based upon organizational and personal values; and
> Designing a "Should" process map to bridge the gap.

Plan the implementation – requires:

> Defining what the logical next steps are;
> Organizing the activities, resources, and timetable;
> Establishing monitoring systems; and
> Developing contingency plans to manage and stabilize the transition.

SYSTEM THEORY

In *The Fifth Discipline*, Senge writes: We've all used the cliché, "I can't see the forest for the trees." Systems Theory is about being able to see the forest and the trees. But unfortunately for most of us, even when we step back we just see lots of trees. Picking one or two and focusing our attention and efforts for change on those is the typical way we do problem solving.

In order to see through the complexity of the forest to the underlying causes that prevent organizations from reaching their ultimate potential, managers must fine tune their systems thinking skills. Managers must not be handcuffed by the complexity. Rather, they must learn to organize potentially complex information into a coherent storyboard that illustrates where current processes are deficient and; therefore, how to improve them. This is not linear problem solving. It is a way to exploit an opportunity to reach a higher level of performance.

Systems thinking can help us in a number of ways. First, it can help us distinguish between changes of relative high importance versus those of relative low importance. Second, it can give us a picture of how changes we implement might affect other components of the system. Third, with a clearer understanding of how our jobs fit into the system, it can help us discover the interrelationships that connect us to the external customers.

The basis of Systems Theory can best be explained by considering examples of systems. Examples, such as:

> ➤ The Solar System
> ➤ The Human Body
> ➤ A Weather System
> ➤ Forests
> ➤ Corporate Structures
> ➤ Patterson's Curse

INPUT-OUTPUT MODEL

One of the most important concepts in creating meaningful change at work is the focus on process. It is process oriented thinking that has enabled our competitors to move ahead in the world economic race. The input-output model is a way of thinking about your job, whatever it might be, in process terms.

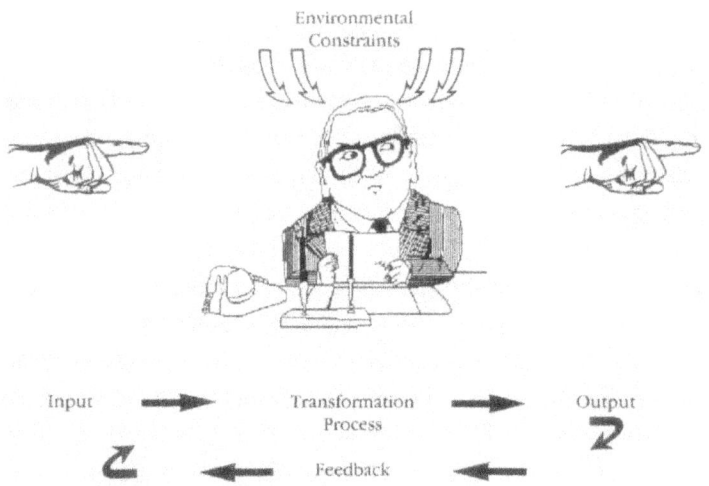

Input - what is put in (i.e. power into a machine, data into a computer, paper, instructions, policies, procedures, etc.)

Inputs can be anything used to get the work done. Here are four general categories:

 ➤ Raw Materials (wood, nails, paper, cloth, grains, rubber, office supplies, etc.)
 ➤ Facilities (rooms, tools, equipment, etc.)
 ➤ Energy (gas, electricity, etc.)
 ➤ Labor (people skills & knowledge)

The quality of the final goods or services is dependent upon high quality inputs.

Transformation Process - a series of changes by which something develops (i.e. the computer program that changes raw data into a finished report)

Transformation Process is the system used to change the inputs into outputs. These methods could include:

➢ Manufacturing Process
➢ Sales and Services Procedures
➢ Accounting Procedures
➢ Medical Procedures

The quality of the final goods or services is dependent upon an unimpaired transformation process.

Output - the work done or amount produced (i.e. the profit/loss statement from the computer, the coffee from the grinder, etc.)

Outputs are what goods or services go to the customer. This may not be the end product. Using the previous examples, the outputs could be as follows:

Transformation Process	Outputs
Manufacturing	Finished Goods
Sales and Service	Repaired Appliance
Accounting	Balance Sheet
Medical	Cured Patient

The customer's satisfaction is dependent upon the quality of the outputs.

Environmental Constraints - confinement or restrictions based on the conditions affecting the system (i.e. laws, budgets, politics, disempowering procedures, etc.)

Environmental constraints may impact all three components of the system. Typically they are negative influences, but they always affect the way one thinks and acts.

Feedback - transfer of a part of the output back to the input, as of electricity or of information.

As a rule, it's important to evaluate the results of our work. Based upon the information received, you could change the input or the way the transformation process works with the intent of improving the output.

This leads to a model for continuous improvement or discovering new business opportunities.

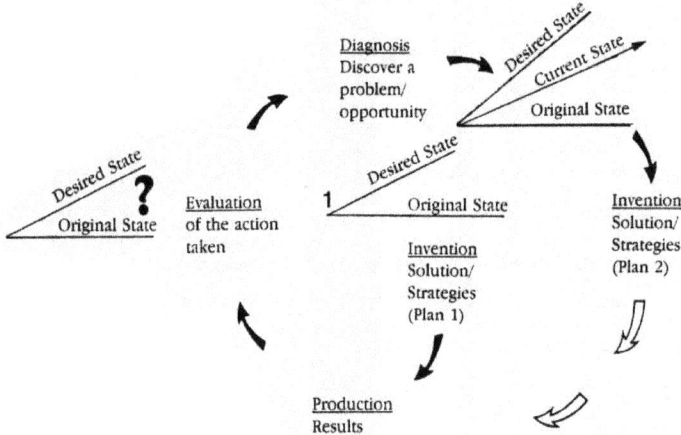

Applying GUIDE to Continuous Improvement

As the leader of an ART, you'll be meeting many times over the life of the continuous improvement project. In this early stage, you will meet to agree on the best project for the team, develop the team's charter, identify the customers, define customer requirements, and finally prepare the "As Is" process map.

*G*ather Information

Ultimately you are looking for the gap between the desired state of the process and what is currently happening. Ask questions about the gap you are trying to close, such as, "What is the problem or opportunity we should be working on?" "Who is the customer for this process?" "What are the customers' requirements?" "How does the process actually flow?"

*U*nderstand the Available Information

The information collected above will depend upon the purpose of the individual meeting. Summarize your understanding of the information discussed before moving on.

*I*nvestigate Alternatives

Seek ideas for the next steps to be completed. For instance, if this is the meeting in which you identified the customers, you should agree on how to determine the customer's requirements. If this is the customer's requirements meeting, then discuss options for developing the "As Is" process map.

*D*ecide on the Best Course of Action, *D*evelop a Plan, and *D*o It

Ask the ART members to agree on who will do what and by when.

*E*valuate Progress and Results, *E*xpress Gratitude

Set a date and time for the next meeting to explore the outcome of the ART assignments. Thank the committee members for their commitment to working on the project.

18

Psychology of Habits and Attitudes

——————————— ⅄ ———————————

INTRODUCTION

The study of the way our minds work and the ensuing behavior is quite a fascinating subject. Our attitudes impact our behavior which becomes habitual based upon our perception of reality. Our self-image is a product of all of our experiences and the way other people react to us. These factors create what becomes our truth; and, we act as if the image were true even if it's not.

Why is it that most people believe they are not creative? Most likely this attitude stems back to the transition from infancy to early childhood. The first years of life are extraordinarily filled with creative learning experiences, from discovering toes and fingers to touching everything within reach. At some point, children begin to experience some constraints, either in the home or at school. The persistently inquisitive "whys" of the two year old are slowly drowned out by the rules of the classroom. Kids were transformed from free-spirited crayon scribblers to "color within the lines" students of order.

When Columbus suggested the world was round, not flat, his ideas flew in the face of all things rational at the time. Galileo was even sent to court to renounce his teachings that the universe revolved around the sun, not the earth. Both were viewed as wild-eyed renegades with no respect for the honored teachings already in place. It doesn't sound all that different than the reception some contemporary individuals receive for suggesting a new procedure at work.

This chapter covers the foundation of current attitudes and how the way people interact with each other affects motivation, work standards, productivity, and the way potential ideas are generated.

In the previous chapter, I defined innovation as the generation of ideas that bring about change. In my experience, many companies give lip service to innovation, but spend little time or money in the pursuit of innovation. A notable exception is 3M, which requires managers to spend ten percent of their time trying to invent new products.

During my classes, I ask students what work related barriers to innovation they experience. In other words, what gets in the way of creativity? Why are you not as creative as possible at work?

Here is a sample of the answers I receive:

➢ People don't like change	➢ Not broke don't fix it
➢ Fear of failure	➢ Not being open to it
➢ Rules	➢ Management discouragement
➢ Takes time	➢ Not getting credit
➢ Not listening	➢ Top people; make changes don't ask
➢ Fear of being wrong	➢ Bureaucracy
➢ New way is difficult	➢ Time
➢ Fear of restructuring	➢ Ideas not accepted
➢ Like the way it is	➢ Not given authority
➢ Beliefs	➢ Copying other companies
➢ Don't like to adapt to new technology	➢ We've always done it that way
➢ More work less pay	➢ Had conflicting goals

Motivations

When you reflect on major or memorable decisions that you have made in your life, were your decisions restrictively motivated or constructively motivated?

Restrictive motivation is based upon fear, you have to do it or else. An example of this type of thinking might be, *if I don't get to work on time, my boss will berate me and give me a poor performance review*. This leads to creative avoidance which manifests in procrastination, absenteeism, sloppy work, no pride of ownership, etc. Clearly when you have an employee who is absent all the time, you should consider this a symptom of a greater problem.

Constructive motivation is based upon desires, personal profitability, and pay value. I teach because it gives me joy. There are no awards, trophies, or recognition that can top the feeling I get when a student comes to me and says, "You changed my life." This leads to self-starting, accepting accountability, increased drive and energy, happiness, etc.

When you lead an ART, it's important that the team members are constructively motivated not restrictively motivated.

Attitudes

Attitudes are based upon your belief system; the assumptions, concepts, values, and practices that constitute the way you view reality. If you believe you can't do something, you won't even try. It's very difficult to bring about meaningful change if you won't even try. What's needed is a paradigm shift.

A paradigm shift is a change in the way you view reality, which leads to disruptive technology. Digital Photography is a perfect example. In January 2012, Kodak filed for Chapter 11 bankruptcy protection, because of disruptive technology. In its hay day Kodak was the best known brand of photographic film products. In 1976, Kodak had an 89% market share of photographic film sales in the United States. I still say, "It's a Kodak moment" when an event demands a photographic record. Ironically, Kodak's Steve Sasson invented the first digital camera.

If you are going to help your company succeed, you'll need an "I Can" attitude. Openness to new ideas is critical to move from VHS to DVD to Blu-ray[tm].

Games People Play

Occasionally, a manager will ask for ideas from the team, but reject them. Worse, if a team member makes suggestions that will help the company improve, some managers criticize the person as well as the idea. I was once told by my supervisor, "Simonds, you're so green, if this building caught on fire, you wouldn't burn."

When the manager says things like, "We've never done it that way." "We haven't the time." "Too expensive..." My favorite, "If it ain't broke, don't fix it." These comments kill the enthusiasm of the employee. Try to avoid blatant criticism, it demoralizes the troops and destroys creative thinking.

The Abilene Paradox

As Jerry Harvey explains it, the Abilene Paradox occurs when organizations take actions contrary to the desires of any of their members and defeat the very purposes they are trying to achieve. Dr. Harvey believes that conflict is not the biggest problem in business, rather not being able to handle agreement is the biggest problem.

The Abilene Paradox manifests in groups when, for example, someone makes a proposal and everyone agrees to the proposed actions. The team members go about completing whatever it is they agreed to do, even though results are not what is expected. Members of the ART keep their negative opinions hidden for fear of being ostracized. They keep plugging away on counterproductive work, which leads to anger, blame, and apparent conflict. But, it's not conflict. Everyone on the team agreed to do something, when no one really wanted to do it in the first place. That is the inability to manage agreement, not conflict.

Groupthink

The psychological drive for consensus at any cost that suppresses disagreement and prevents the appraisal of alternatives in cohesive decision-making groups is how Janis (1982) defines groupthink. In other words, when group members use a mode of thinking in which their striving for agreement overrides their ability to realistically appraise alternative courses of action, negative consequences are highly probable.

This phenomenon occurs when groups meet with the purpose of reaching agreement. As the leader of an ART, you might start a meeting by saying, "The purpose of this meeting is to agree on the best way to proceed on the XYZ project...." Inadvertently, you have told your team that you want them to agree "to proceed" regardless of any misgivings they may have about the project. Consequently, team members self-censor their objections in order to live up to the group's expectations.

Summary

Based upon my literature review, I synthesized the barriers to creativity and innovation into four types:

1. Fear
2. Self-limiting paradigms
3. Overly judgmental team members
4. Group dynamics phenomenon

Awareness of these barriers is the first step in changing these detrimental habits and attitudes. Achievement of group goals is dependent upon the ART members utilizing a variety of prevention strategies. Using GUIDE as a meeting agenda and CARE to maintain relationships will go a long way to encourage team members to stay on task. Other prevention techniques include:

1. Encouraging open-mindedness
2. Assigning a critical evaluator role
3. Challenging conventional wisdom
4. Disclosing feelings and hopes to encourage trust
5. Allowing risk taking

The next chapter will cover techniques to achieve success in groups and some creative thinking methodologies.

19

Techniques of Group Process and Creative Thinking Methodology

———————————— ⅄ ————————————

INTRODUCTION

Since this section emphasizes Action Research Teams, it is important to consider the way people interact in group settings. Action Research has been previously defined as a method for gaining win-win outcomes. The most effective Action Research Teams involve members who have nothing to gain or lose through their participation. Although this is not mandatory, it does seem to be the best method to be employed.

In *A Collaborative Action Research: A Developmental Approach*, Oja and Smulyan emphasize the effective Action Research experience requires open communication, collaboration, adequate time and resources, and a commitment to the concept of parity in order to be successful and effective.

My graduate advisor, Oscar Mink, adds Action Research is a cyclical process in which groups make a conscious effort to analyze the problems they are facing, identify the cause of their problem, reach a mutual agreement on the solution, test the solution proposed by actually taking action to correct the problem and continually adjust their findings in light of feedback in order to solve real problems and to facilitate the growth and better functioning of their organization. This requires three important concepts: 1) division of labor, 2) developmental thinking, and 3) interactive skill.

Division of Labor

There are essentially three roles required for Action Research Teams to work well. The first one is Process Facilitator. The Process Facilitator is the person leading the meeting and has the primary responsibility to manage group dynamics in a structured fashion. This person has no ownership of the problem and consequently can be very objective in the management of group process.

The second important role is the Client. The Client owns the problem and has the responsibility to make decisions regarding the course of action taken or the responsibility to implement the decision once the meeting is over.

All other members of the group will be Resources for the Client. The purpose of Resources is to provide ideas and intellectual discussion about the meeting subject. Additionally, Resources may provide administrative help for the Process Facilitator; such as, keeping time and recording important facts for group memory.

The Process Facilitator develops an agenda utilizing the Client's input that includes:

1. Desired Outcomes – A statement such as, By the end of this meeting we will have:
   - A clear understanding of the cause of the problem
   - Selected the best solution to the problem
   - Created an implementation schedule

2. Choice of Decision Making Methods – such as:
   - Consensus
   - With a fall back to weighted voting

3. Ground Rules – which usually include such things as:
   - Respect others
   - Listen with full attention

4. Roles and Responsibilities – such as:
   - Scribe
   - Time Keeper

5. Meeting Content and Process -
   GUIDE   Process Steps   Lead   Time

Developmental Thinking vs. Decision Making Thinking

It is important to differentiate between developmental thinking and decision making thinking. When the Action Research Team is trying to invent solutions, critical comments can thwart the creativity of the group. When the Team moves into the implementation planning phase, critical evaluation is sought to avoid going to Abilene or Groupthink.

Developmental Thinking

1. Inventing, using a child's curiosity, fantasizing, exploring many points of view;
2. Building on ideas, giving credit, valuing & respecting people;

---

3. Thinking of and listing attributes or advantages first;
4. Replacing killer phrases with "How to…," "I wish…," or "Could we…?" phrases.

Decision Making Thinking

1. Avoid evaluating too early;
2. Seek logical conclusions;
3. Ask Client for major concerns;
4. Seek modifications from Resources;
5. Ask Client to make a decision by asking questions about newness, feasibility, next steps, and commitment.

Developmental Reply

The next important concept is the Developmental Reply. Let's say you are in an Action Research meeting and you ask team members for ideas on how to solve the problem at hand. As ideas are suggested, it is human nature to evaluate those ideas immediately. You make a decision based upon where the idea falls on a continuum from worthless to perfect.

The closer it is to perfect the more you like it. The closer it is to worthless the more you hate it and the more inclined you are to reject it out right.

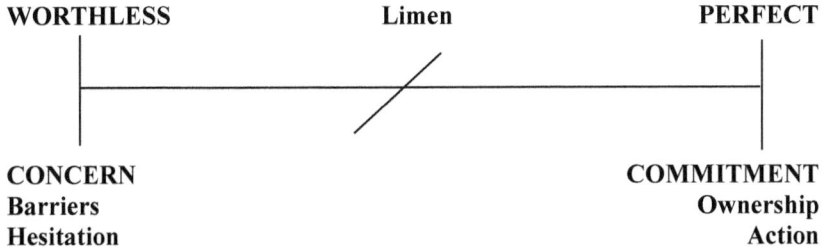

WORTHLESS   Limen   **PERFECT**

CONCERN   **COMMITMENT**
Barriers   **Ownership**
Hesitation   **Action**

Limen - The point at which a stimulus is of sufficient intensity to begin to produce an effect.

When you are in the developmental phase of the meeting and an idea falls to the left of your personal limen, don't reject it. Rather, use the Developmental Reply.

Start by paraphrasing your understanding of the idea. It is important that the originator acknowledges that you fully understand it before continuing. Then offer two or three positive observations of the idea. State what and why you like a part of the idea. It might sound like this:

1. "I like that it would meet the customers' expectations."
2. "I think it would be a relatively inexpensive fix."
3. "It definitely would improve the quality of the product."

Then add the part that bothers you, like this, "My only concern is how it will effect cycle time."

Finally ask the person or group to modify the idea in such a way as to keep the plusses and change the concern. You could say, "How can we modify the idea to overcome the concern?"

By using the Developmental Reply, you will maintain the positive nature of the creative part of the meeting and soon your team will bring ideas to the table that are already to the right of your limen.

Applying GUIDE to Generating Solutions Meeting

As the leader of an ART you'll be meeting many times over the life of the continuous improvement project. In the middle stage you will meet to measure variation, document data collection, generate solutions, select the best solution, and finally design the "Should Be" process map.

*G*ather Information

Ultimately you are looking for the solution to close the gap between the desired state of the process and what is currently happening. If the Client is present, ask that person to describe, "What do you want to accomplish?" "Why are we here?" "What has been tried?" "Is there anything you'd like us to include or exclude from our thinking?"

*U*nderstand the Available Information

The information collected above will depend upon the purpose of the individual meeting. Summarize your understanding of the information discussed before moving on.

*I*nvestigate Alternatives

Use developmental thinking concepts. Pick one of the creative thinking methods from the next section and use it. If the Client is present, let that person choose one of the ideas to explore further. Try another one. Repeat until the Client says, "That's the idea I want to use."

*D*ecide on the Best Course of Action, *D*evelop a Plan, and *D*o It

Ask the Client to use the developmental reply to summarize likes. Seek any concerns and ask the Resources to modify the idea. Ask the Client for commitment to action.

*E*valuate Progress and Results, *E*xpress Gratitude

Set a date and time for the next meeting to explore the outcome of the ART members' assignments. Thank the committee members for their commitment to working on the project.

CREATIVE THINKING METHODOLOGY

Most people are full of ideas, insights and experiences that can improve their work area and their organization as a whole. They are rich with the ability to see systems, tasks, and people from a unique perspective. Coffee breaks and the employee lunch table probably generate more ideas for improving organizations than any staff meeting. Why? The informal gatherings are "safe." Employees inventory problems, talk about how things should be done and never feel threatened, bogged down by analysis, or embarrassed if told "that's ridiculous." The secret to developing creativity and innovation is to replicate the coffee break.

Employees need the freedom to take the risk of surfacing new ideas. They need to know it's safe to challenge the way things have been done in the past. The only way to open the floodgates of new ideas is to create an atmosphere of safety.

Four Levels of Creativity		
Adapting	Modifying Style	Can we adapt what we already have?
Combining	Experimental Style	What combinations can we come up with?
Inventing	Visioning Style	Can we imagine the ideal solution?
Originating	Exploring Style	Can we create something from nothing?

Although there are many methods for creativity, learning ways to look at problems from different points of view is important. In the following pages are ten of the most useful creative thinking methods.

Movie Magic

In this technique, you are going to create a scene, like a motion picture, that helps you solve the problem. For example, you might think of a problem statement like, "We need to decrease the machine down time in the plant."

Now relax. Forget about the problem. In your mind, go to your favorite serene vacation spot. Close your eyes. This is one of mine:

There is a lovely place in the Great Smokey Mountains National Park called Cade's Cove where I go in my mind to relax when feeling stressed. Imagine you are driving through the mountains. You notice the trees and rugged terrain; but when you enter the cove, it is soft, peaceful. You can smell the grass and flowers if the dogwoods are in bloom. You feel the cool breeze, a perfect temperature. You can hear water trickling from Laurel Creek. You look toward the sound and see Cable Mill. You walk into the mill and see an old Tennessee mill grinder. He speaks to you. You create a dialogue with him. You tell him your work related problem and he gives you a suggestion. You ask him to clarify anything you want to know, and he does. You acknowledge his contribution to your thinking and shake his hand. You leave the mill and stretch out on the cool, soft grass of the cove. As you relax, you simply go over in your mind what the old-timer has told you. You test it and modify it to meet your needs.

Come out of Cade's Cove slowly. Open your eyes. Note anything that might help you solve your problem.

Brainstorming

Alex Osborn developed the approach known as brainstorming in 1938. Many people misuse the technique today by trying to utilize it for all problem solving. It implies a hit and miss form of creativity which may have been effective in the advertising world for which it was designed. Although it is not the most effective of the techniques discussed in this section, Process Facilitators are taught how to use brainstorming effectively and to combine it with other methods. Here are the characteristics most people consider when they use the technique:

> ➤ Record as many ideas as you can
> ➤ Suspend evaluation
> ➤ Stretch - aim for quantity
> ➤ Accept all ideas, especially the wild ones
> ➤ Encourage building on ideas

Animation Exercise

Animation means to give life or motion to. There are four different types of animation:

First, a personal animation is one in which you try to become something else. For instance, if there have been a number of complaints from doctors over delays in diagnostic reports, I could ask someone to become the MRI equipment and ask how he spends his day? How does she feel about herself? How does he feel about his job? What does she see going on around her?

Second, an example of direct animation would be looking at something in another field and applying it directly to the problem. For instance, in *The Creative Edge*, Miller uses the example that the inspiration for Velcro came from observing how burdock burrs cling to clothing.

Third, a symbolic animation uses an incorrect image. For instance, (something) that (performs a function) like a (something else). For example, you might want to invent a new paint that repairs nicks automatically, like your skin heals.

Fourth, a fanciful animation would be most like the movie magic technique. For instance, you might take yourself on a voyage to Mars to try to find the solution to a design flaw in an aircraft plant.

Preferences

This technique is taken from the field of negotiating. Preferences simply means looking at options for solving a problem. For instance, I might ask in a meeting, "Do you prefer a steel casing or would a lighter material have advantages?"

Oxymoron

An oxymoron is a paradox. Jumbo shrimp, military intelligence, and postal service are examples. Creating an oxymoron that describes an important part of the problem, provides distance from the forest so you can see the trees.

This technique is typically used in conjunction with other techniques. For example, I might ask for an oxymoron from the group and once there are enough collected, use the most intriguing oxymoron to springboard us into a Time Machine.

Thought starters:

Youthfully – Old
Safely – Dangerous
Losing – Gains
Trustingly – Suspicious
Publicly – Private
Fully – Empty
Quickly – Slow

Time Machine

Taking a journey to a different place in time creates distance from the problem as well. For instance, I might ask you for examples of indestructibility in the world of the American west to get you to think of solutions to vandalism today.

The technique is most effective if you use an inanimate system when working on a personnel problem and a human system when working on an object or process related problem.

Inanimate Systems	Human Systems
Geology	Victorian England
Astrology	The Renaissance
Electronics	World War II
Forestry	Biology or Physiology

Expert Perspectives

Since one of the characteristics of creative thought is the ability to look at problems from many points of view, force that to happen.

The facilitator of a group problem-solving meeting might suggest looking at the problem from a consultant's point of view. Other questions might be, "What would your clergyman say was the solution?", "How would a lawyer try to resolve this?" etc.

Force Field Analysis

The theoretical foundation for force field analysis was developed by Kurt Lewin in 1951. It assumes that the system is in a state of equilibrium between forces working for the change and forces working against the change. The technique involves an examination of the forces that are contributing to or hindering a solution and then developing ways of removing or reducing the restraining forces, increasing the contributing forces, or both. The contributing forces are allowed to move the system easily in the desired direction.

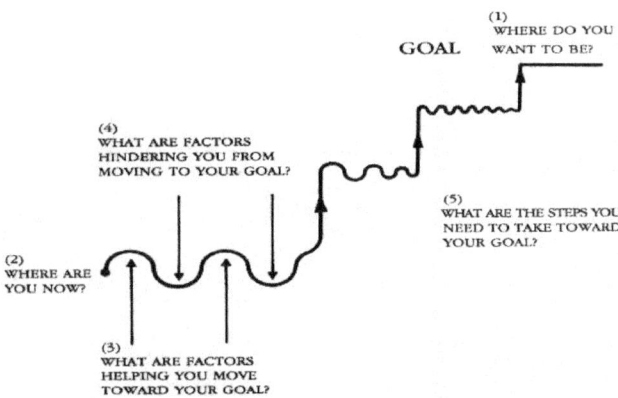

Features and Benefits

An analogy from the field of selling: think of yourself as a salesman and you've got to describe all the features and benefits of your product. Focus on your problem. List all the features and then ask, "How can I make the feature more beneficial?" For instance, "How can I make the features lighter, faster, stronger, cheaper, more efficient or effective?"

By listing the features, you can then figure out how to substitute other materials, combine purposes, or modify the current situation. You might eliminate, magnify, reverse, or rearrange the components of the system or process.

Fantastic Solutions

Select one intriguing conclusion from an animation exercise and ask the members of the group to think of a solution that is so preposterous that it could get you fired. Once the idea is voiced, the Process Facilitator should ask, "What images does this create for others in the group and how could you build on this idea?" The result should be a list of potential dream solutions.

Thought starters:

- How to make this more expensive?
- How to make this plan fail?
- How to make upper management hate it?
- How to make it more complicated?
- How to make others doubt it?
- How to make morale worse?

20

Project Management

INTRODUCTION

Once an Action Research Team helps its Client develop creative solutions or ideas to help improve the organization, the Client is responsible for implementing those ideas. In order to ensure that creative ideas are successful, it's appropriate to develop a project plan.

This chapter covers the six phases of Project Management. They are:

1. Define the problem or opportunity
2. Plan the project activities
3. Determine personnel needs and work assignments
4. Establish management control methods
5. Reach group consensus
6. Conclude the project and document results

Define the Problem or Opportunity

To achieve the best results with your project, it will be important to define the project in terms of goals and objectives. See Setting Objectives in Chapter 2.

The next step in the Define stage is to gather information and organize it. Most of the information that you'll need can be categorized in one of four ways. To help you organize all necessary data systematically, you'll want to attempt to write down everything you're aware of about the current situation.

The four categories are:

Assumptions - to take for granted. For instance, you may take for granted that you will have management support for these projects.

Guidelines - a principle by which to determine a course of action. There are organizational policies and procedures which must be followed. How will these affect this project?

Resources - something ready for use or available as needed. These would include raw materials, facilities, energy, labor and money.

Tasks - a piece of work to be done. This means listing the steps required to accomplish the project.

Plan the Project Activities

In the development of the actual plan, there will be a number of action steps. For instance, you will need to identify all project activities, estimate time and cost, sequence the task, allocate resources and develop contingency plans.

During the Define stage, tasks were listed that need to be completed but may not have been in any particular sequence. As a first step to developing the plan, determine the inter-dependence of the activities. For instance, it might be appropriate to design the specifications of a peer training course before ordering the materials to be used in the course. Some actions can be started only after others have been completed.

Next, allocate the resources. Depending upon the complexity of the project you've selected, you may need additional labor. In which case, you will want to seek help from other members of the team. Otherwise, the allocation of resources can be listed on the Planning form, as needed.

The third step in developing the plan is to establish the schedule. Although there are many ways of doing this, start by working backwards by establishing the finishing date and then charting the schedule of events using a Gantt format.

A critical review of the plan, at this step in the process, is important. There may be potential risks for which contingencies need to be developed. Start this part of the process by asking, "If anything could go wrong, what would it be?" "Where might there be potential delays in the plan?"

Next, you will want to differentiate between small and high risk. This can be done by determining the probability of the potential problem occurring and assessing the magnitude of the adverse consequences should the potential problem occur. For instance, you might ask yourself, "What is the likelihood that this problem will actually happen?" then ask, "If it does happen, will the impact be severe?"

Finally, you will want to establish courses of action that will minimize the effects if the problem should occur.

Page 190 shows a sample Project Management Planning Form including the tasks (in general terms), resources, and a twelve week schedule. The recommendation is to select a project that can be completed within a twelve week period. If you select a project that will take significantly longer time, the probability of it being completed goes down. Starting with a small project, especially for your first one, increases the probability of success. Once your confidence is built, go for another project with more complexity.

PROJECT MANAGEMENT PLANNING FORM

Define The Problem Or Opportunity: *Implement Change at Work*

TASKS	Raw Materials	Facilities	Energy	Labor	Money	Drop Dead Date	WEEKLY SCHEDULE 1 2 3 4 5 6 7 8 9 10 11 12
			RESOURCES				
1. Select a Project	None	Room # 222	Lights	Me		Week #	
2. Select a Team			..	..			
3. Develop Team Charter		Yes	..	Team		Week 1	
4. Identify Customers			..	..			
5. Define Customer Requirements			..	..		Week # 3	
6. "As Is" Process Map	Drawing paper	Larg Mtg Rm	..	Bob / Team / B..& L			
7. Measure Variation			..	..		Week #5	
8. Document Data Collection	Computer	Lrg Mtg Rm	..	..		Week	
9. Generate Solutions			..	Team		Week #	
10. Select Best Solution							
11. Design "Should Be" Map	Drawing paper	..		..	Budget $10,000	Week #8	
12. Test Hypothesis							
13. Develop Implementation Procedures	Paper/ supplies Forms					Weeks 8-12	
14. Document Results							
15. Celebrate	Party Supplies	Hotel Ballroom				Week 12	

CONTINGENCIES *If cost runs over $10,000 - document potential ROI & get approval*

Determine Personnel Needs and Work Assignments

Having completed and documented the plan, it is now time to begin implementing the plan. You'll need to make some decisions at this point about who will do the work. You will need to prepare work assignments and fit them into your schedule. If you do have someone to whom you may delegate, you will still want to prepare the work assignments in basically the same way. The difference would be that you would have to gain the commitment of others and establish monitoring systems for them.

In developing the work assignments, you should take each task listed on the Planning Sheet and break it down answering the following questions:

The Nature of the Work

"What work is to be done on this task?"

"How much time is needed to complete the work?"

"Why is effective performance important in this work?"

"What is my responsibility?"

Performance Standards

"What are the performance standards (quality, quantity, deadlines, cost) for this activity?"

"How can performance be measured?"

"What are the restrictions and are they negotiable?"

Delegated Authority

"What amount of decision making authority do I have?"

"How frequently do I have to involve my boss?"

Potential Barriers

"What concerns or issues should I discuss with the boss?"

"What potential barriers might inhibit performance?"

"What actions can be taken to overcome the barriers?"

Monitoring Progress

"What control information is needed?"

"When and how often is information needed?"

"Who should review it?"

Establish Management Control Methods

Management control methods constitute the way a project manager monitors what's going on. These control mechanisms go hand-in-hand with the planning process. Whereas, in planning, the focus is on large tasks while in controlling, the focus is concerned more with precision and attention to the details.

You should set up various control methods for each of the resources in your plan. The following are examples of some of them:

Raw Materials
- ➢ Purchasing policies and procedures
- ➢ Inventory control systems

Facilities
- ➢ Housekeeping report
- ➢ Leasing information
- ➢ Inventory of equipment and tools
- ➢ Maintenance report

Energy
- ➢ Electric bills
- ➢ Gas bills
- ➢ Water bills

Labor
- ➢ Performance appraisals
- ➢ Safety records
- ➢ Productivity or status reports

Money
- ➢ Budgets
- ➢ Financial reports
- ➢ Vendor quotations

Reach Group Consensus

There will be times when the Action Research Team will help in the implementation of the project or another intact team may be required. Because people do not always agree, it is important to utilize one of several techniques for reaching group consensus.

Consensus is defined as *general* agreement, which implies that some members of the team may not agree. However, all members of the team should feel that their ideas were heard and the decision was reached fairly. This leads to a sense of commitment to the decision.

Consensus *is not* voting. Although many teams have used voting, it usually leads to someone winning and someone else losing.

In a consensus meeting, the meeting leader should strive to allow every person's opinion to be heard before beginning the selection process. The leader should look for ways to organize the items or to prioritize them. Once ready to select, the team should be committed to selecting an option that is acceptable to everyone. Here are some ways of reaching the decision:

Benjamin Franklin's Balance Sheet

This technique is used when trying to decide whether to do something or not to do it. List the pros and cons of implementing the idea on a flip chart or sheet of paper. Once everyone has agreed that all the pros and cons are listed, the leader suggests that the longer list wins. If there are more pros, do it; more cons, don't.

Criteria-Based Decision

This technique is most useful when trying to decide among a moderate number of options, not more than five. First, list down the left hand side of a flip chart or piece of paper all the essential criteria. Essential criteria are those that would be automatic knock-outs if one of the alternatives did not have it. Then, list all the useful criteria underneath the essential criteria. Useful criteria would be nice-to-have, but are not knock-out criteria. You may want to assign a value to the useful criteria; such as, high-medium-low, or use a ten-point scale.

Now list all the alternatives across the top of the paper. Compare all the essential criteria to the way the alternative meets it. Then compare the useful criteria to the way the alternative meets it. The alternative that wins is the one that passes all the essential criteria and meets the useful ones the best.

Weighted Voting

This technique is most suited when the group has many options to choose from, usually five to ten. Each member of the team is allowed a pre-established number of votes. Usually the number of votes is twice the number of items on the list.

Each team member may distribute the allowed votes within the following constraints:

> ➢ no more than 50% on any one item
> ➢ voting for at least half of the items
> ➢ must use all votes allocated

Then, the leader makes a matrix on the flip chart and calculates the weighted average. The option with the most votes wins.

Weighted Ranking

This technique is most useful in reducing the number of things the group will try to do. For instance, the group has a ten item list and has agreed to do only the top four items. Each team member is allocated ten votes. Members place a 10 beside the one project they would most like to do. Then, place a 1 beside the item of least interest. A 9 goes beside the second most intriguing and a 2 beside the second least interesting. This continues toward the middle until all numbers have been used.

The leader calculates the weighted average and posts the top four options.

This technique can also be used to prioritize a list of activities, when the team intends to do all the items on the list.

Conclude the Project and Document Results

Although it is important for each project to have a conclusion date, it has been said repeatedly that Action Research is a continuous process. Therefore, what should happen next may seem contradictory.

At the conclusion of the project:

- ➢ Attain the Client's acceptance of the proposed solution;
- ➢ Install the change permanently;
- ➢ Establish a maintenance plan;
- ➢ Document the project;
- ➢ Integrate into the cultural system; and
- ➢ Issue a final report.

An annual review could include a diagnosis of any needed changes or enhancements to the process. This would lead us to another invention cycle in the Action Research Model. If, for any reason, you are unable to continue this process yourself, it would be appropriate to train an insider to take over the functions that you have initiated.

Section Six

Managing
Performance

21

Developing Performance Results Categories and Objectives

---------------------------- ⅄ ----------------------------

INTRODUCTION

Congratulations! If you've stuck with me this far, you now have the skills you need for *Achieving on Purpose*. Section Six summarizes everything that you've learned. This is the essence of your GUIDE to Managerial Success.

Managing performance is an important supervisory skill. Leaders are charged with the responsibility of getting things done through others. This section will help you establish a systematic approach to ensure that direct reports are meeting or exceeding their performance expectations.

This chapter covers preparatory work for the following behavioral competencies:

Establishing Reporting Systems – Setting up procedures to monitor activities needed to succeed in the job. Steps include:

> ➢ Identifying what information needs to be obtained
> ➢ Collecting pertinent information in a timely manner
> ➢ Reviewing reports to track work progress
> ➢ Encouraging employees to maintain their own quality control charts

Developing Performance Standards – Using appropriate interpersonal styles to guide the development of work expectations:

> ➢ Clarifying expected performance, goals, and objectives
> ➢ Seeking involvement from the employee
> ➢ Gaining genuine agreement and enthusiasm for targets
> ➢ Documenting the plan for tracking purposes

The objective of using GUIDE for Managing Performance is to ensure that people understand what is expected of them in terms of quality, quantity, timeliness and cost. It is important because associates need to be working on the right things which meet the objectives of the organization, department, and work team.

The benefits of using GUIDE for Managing Performance are to:

> Improve productivity
> Increase employee ownership of the work
> Increase employee self-motivation
> Decrease wasted effort

The cycle begins with defining performance clearly. Most jobs can be realistically described within the framework of three to seven functional areas called Performance Results Categories (PRCs).

For example: A sales person might be evaluated on how well he:

1. Manages the assigned territory
2. Acquires new accounts or the associated sales volume
3. Satisfies customers
4. Develops product knowledge
5. Maintains inter-departmental relations

Start the *Achieving on Purpose* cycle by preparing Goals and Standards.

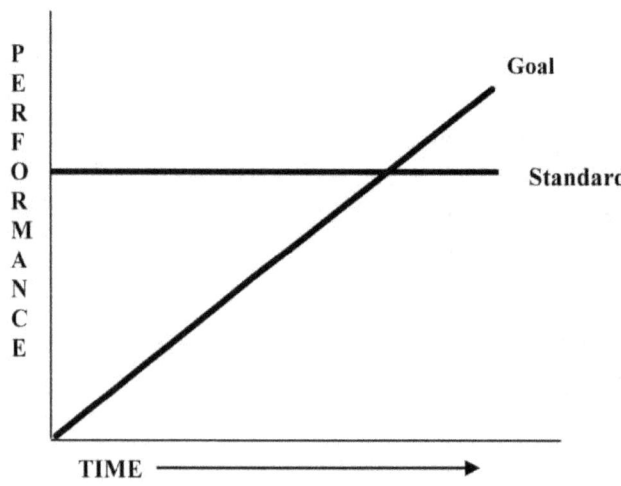

Applying GUIDE to Performance Results Categories

Using GUIDE while preparing your PRCs helps keep you focused on the task and ensures that you proceed efficiently to the desired outcomes. What follows is a description of each component of the GUIDE model within the context of developing your Performance Results Categories.

Gather Information

The first step in developing PRCs is to gather as much information as you can about the position. Gathering the following types of information is most helpful in this stage of the process:

> - Previous job descriptions
> - Previous performance appraisals
> - Letters and memos
> - Reports
> - Your leaders PRCs

There are three things to keep in mind when defining a job. First, you have a job because your boss has more responsibility than can be handled alone. She delegates authority to you to reach the company's objectives and mission. Therefore, you should know what those are and prepare yours accordingly.

Second, you are attempting to reduce your job to its smallest common denominator. In other words, you are selecting the PRCs that best describe the meaningful outcomes of your job, which are measurable, and reflect organizational values.

Third, you will want to consider what resources are available to help you reach the desired outcomes.

Understand the Available Information

Confirming understanding when developing your PRCs means double-checking your sources by:

> - Asking questions about the documents you have collected
> - Confirming the details are accurate
> - Finding out what tools, methods, and other resources are at your disposal

As with gathering information, confirming understanding is not something you do once. As you get additional information and formulate new ideas, you should cycle back and confirm your understanding.

At the conclusion of this step you are ready to generate a tentative list of PRCs.

*I*nvestigate Alternatives

At this stage of developing your PRCs, you will want to generate a list of alternatives. The list should include all the meaningful, measurable things you do on a regular basis.

The PRCs should be in the form of short phrases like:

> ➢ Forecasting
> ➢ Staff Development
> ➢ Sales Support
> ➢ Volunteer Orientation
> ➢ Personal and Professional Development

Shoot for up to fourteen at the most. Too few will not clearly define your position and too many alternatives can lead to analysis paralysis and unnecessary confusion.

*D*ecide on the Best Course of Action, *D*evelop a Plan, and *D*o It

Now it is time to examine the list of alternatives and to reduce it to three to seven, with five being optimal.

No one has a crystal ball. The goal is to simplify complexity, reduce uncertainty and resolve conflict which leads to better decisions.

*E*valuate Progress and Results, *E*xpress Gratitude

At this stage in the process, evaluate means to double-check your PRCs against the following checklist:

> ➢ Do these describe the meaningful outcomes of the job?
> ➢ Are they unchanging?
> ➢ Do they reflect company values?

Evaluating progress and results enables you to correct mistakes and confirm success.

PRC - Areas and Methods of Measurement

Performance expectations should be in writing and include some form of measurement with respect to quality, quantity, timeliness, and cost. The result would include at least one measurement from each area. Ideally, the result would include all four. The more expectations are defined, the easier it is to hit the target. See Setting Objectives in Chapter 2.

Using the easiest example, let's take our salesperson's second Performance Results Category:

PRC	Area of Measurement	Method
Acquires new accounts or the associated sales volume	Quality	Number of products returned
	Quantity	Sales Revenue Generated
	Timeliness	Close sales within X days
	Cost	Budget < Y% of Revenue

Applying GUIDE to SMART Performance Objectives

Gather Information

The first step in identifying SMART objectives is to gather as much information as you can about the position. Gathering the following types of information is most helpful in this stage of the process:

- ➢ Previous objective worksheets
- ➢ Previous performance appraisals
- ➢ Letters and memos
- ➢ Reports
- ➢ Your leader's objectives

Understand the Available Information

Use the exact methods to confirm understanding of your SMART objectives as you did with the PRCs, namely:

- ➢ Asking questions about the documents you have collected
- ➢ Confirming the details are accurate
- ➢ Finding out what tools, methods, and other resources are at your disposal

At the conclusion of this step you are ready to generate a tentative list of SMART objectives.

Investigate Alternatives

At this stage of identifying your SMART objectives, you will want to generate a list of alternatives. The list should include two or three ways of accomplishing each PRC.

Example alternatives for our sales person might be:

- ➢ To produce $500,000 in sales revenue in 12 months
- ➢ To acquire three new accounts per quarter
- ➢ To balance product mix across all lines by year-end

GUIDE offers various techniques and tools for generating alternatives. The techniques used to generate alternatives will depend on the context of the situation. In the case of SMART objectives, it is best to simply brainstorm a list based upon your research in the Gather stage.

Decide on the Best Course of Action, Develop a Plan, and Do It

Now it is time to examine the list of alternatives and to reduce it to a reasonable, viable, and manageable number, perhaps three to five.

Evaluate Progress and Results, Express Gratitude

At this stage in the process, evaluate means to double-check your objectives against the SMART checklist:

> ➢ Are they Specific?
> ➢ Are they Measurable?
> ➢ Are they Attainable?
> ➢ Are they Realistic?
> ➢ Are they Time bound?

The resulting effective goal statement would be:

"To produce $500,000 in sales revenue in 12 months, while keeping returns under 2%, closing sales within 45 days, and limiting expenses to 4% of revenue."

Means to Attaining SMART Objectives

Successful fulfillment of the desired outcomes is contingent on how a person behaves. Not only do workers need to know what the performance expectation is, they need to know the skills or actions that will be needed to achieve it.

Often leaders fail to make the desired behavior a part of the SMART objectives discussion. By discussing the means to attaining the desired result, you will increase the probability of success.

If our sales person is going to reach the target of $500,000 in sales revenue, she will have to call a certain number of prospects, qualify leads, articulate customer needs, demonstrate capability to satisfy those needs, write proposals, negotiate deliverables, etc.

For example:

SMART Objectives	Behavioral Objectives
To produce $500,000 in sales revenue in 12 months, while keeping returns under 2%, closing sales within 45 days, and limiting expenses to 4% of revenue.	Initiate 10 phone calls per day Schedule 20 face-to-face calls per month Write two proposals per week

Double-check your Behavioral Objectives against the following checklist:

> ➢ Are they related to the SMART Objectives?
> ➢ Are they observable, trackable behaviors?
> ➢ Are they attainable?

22

Gaining Commitment to Performance Expectations

INTRODUCTION

It is important to involve your direct reports in developing their own performance expectations. This will go a long way toward building commitment and ownership of the job. People will try harder and be more dedicated to accomplishing those results for which they have full agreement.

This chapter covers the interactive components of the following behavioral competencies:

Establishing Reporting Systems – Setting up procedures to monitor activities needed to succeed in the job. Steps include:

- ➢ Identifying what information needs to be obtained
- ➢ Collecting pertinent information in a timely manner
- ➢ Reviewing reports to track work progress
- ➢ Encouraging employees to maintain their own quality control charts

Developing Performance Standards – Using appropriate interpersonal styles to guide the development of work expectations:

- ➢ Clarifying expected performance, goals, and objectives
- ➢ Seeking involvement from the employee
- ➢ Gaining genuine agreement and enthusiasm for targets
- ➢ Documenting the plan for tracking purposes

It will be necessary to educate your people about the process. This will undoubtedly require a meeting and could involve some coaching prior to finalizing the expected performance. You will want to take them through the exercises that you went through in the previous chapter. If you just hired this person, it might be appropriate to show him the job qualifications you used to make the hiring decision, as a starting point.

Ask each person to prepare a list of PRCs, Measurements, SMART Objectives, and Behavioral Objectives. Coach your reports to use GUIDE, as you did. Schedule a meeting within a reasonable period of time. One week ought to be sufficient.

In the *Achieving on Purpose* cycle you are now at the point of Gaining Commitment to Performance Expectations.

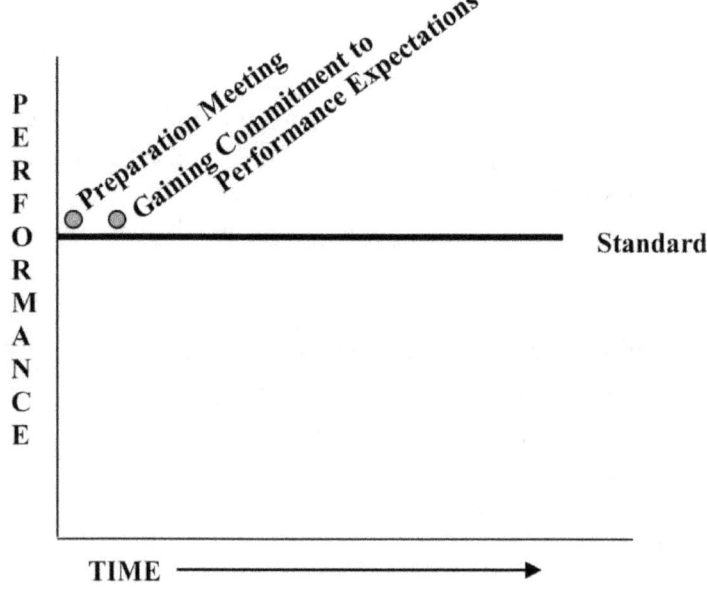

Applying GUIDE to Gaining Commitment to Performance Expectations

There are two options for using GUIDE in this meeting. One is to follow GUIDE for the PRCs, then go back and start over for the SMART Objectives, etc. The other is to take one PRC at a time and complete the SMART Objectives, Behavioral Objectives, and Monitoring decisions for that one and then go back for PRC number two, etc. What follows is a description of each component of the GUIDE model in the context of Gaining Commitment.

𝐺ather Information

The first step in gaining commitment to performance expectations is to gather as much information as you can about the situation. In this case, you have asked this person to prepare in advance; so, the first thing to do is ask for an explanation of that preparation.

Be prepared to take your time. You will want to ask the person, tentatively, what she wants to accomplish in the coming year and be prepared to ask follow-up questions like:

> "How did you plan to accomplish that?"
> "What help were you thinking I might provide?"
> "What resources did you consider using?"

When you have solicited the information you desired; move on to the next step.

𝑈nderstand the Available Information

In this meeting confirming understanding means being sure that you know what the employee's goals are for the coming year. The techniques are the same as in other meetings, only the content has changed:

- ➢ Repeat or summarize the information collected
- ➢ Check for agreement on the details
- ➢ Ask the employee to state his understanding and compare it to yours

At the conclusion of this step you both should have a clear understanding of the tentative plan.

𝐼nvestigate Alternatives

To be sure, there are times when the choices are very limited or when the employee has done an excellent job in preparing. In those situations, you may be better off simply agreeing to the alternatives and moving to the next step in GUIDE.

However, if you think there may be other alternatives or the person hasn't considered a potential pitfall, this is where you would offer your ideas.

If you can accept the employee's ideas, she will be committed to carrying them out. On the other hand, if you cannot, then you must present your idea as an alternative.

*D*ecide on the Best Course of Action, *D*evelop a Plan, and *D*o It

At this stage, you will want to finalize the PRCs, SMART Objectives, and Behavioral Objectives. Then you will want to decide on tracking methods and frequency. In many cases a tracking mechanism is already in place; such as, monthly sales reports that show the revenue generated, production reports, financial statements, etc.

You might say something like:

> "Okay, we have agreement on your goals for the year...Now do we have a mechanism for tracking it? What would you suggest?" And then, "How frequently should we review progress?"

Remember the goal is to simplify complexity, reduce uncertainty and resolve conflict, which leads to better decisions.

*E*valuate Progress and Results, *E*xpress Gratitude

At the conclusion of this meeting, there will be no results to measure. You will want to set a date for your next meeting and express gratitude. Expressing gratitude acknowledges contributions and ceremoniously brings this GUIDE journey to an end.

You might say something like:

> "Why don't we meet next month, say the 3rd at 9:00 A.M. to review progress? I'm confident that you'll be able to complete these expectations successfully. Thanks for the hard work?"

Positive Model: Gaining Commitment to Performance Expectations

Gaining commitment to performance expectations can be very rewarding. Here is a sample of what might happen during this type of discussion for a Training Manager.

Gather information:

> **Leader** – Bob, I'm very excited about working with you to establish performance expectations for the coming year. It's important that we agree on what's to be accomplished and how you'll get there. This discussion will help you understand the job, how the performance can be tracked, and the way we'll evaluate your success. Your input in the process is valuable; I'm counting on your active participation.
>
> **Bob** – I'm ready with my preparation.
>
> **Leader** – Great! I thought we'd take one PRC at a time, discuss the SMART Objectives and the Behavioral Objectives, come to an agreement and then come back to the next PRC. Does that sound Okay? How do you feel about the process?
>
> **Bob** – Fine, it makes sense.
>
> **Leader** – Why don't you tell me what you prepared for your first PRC?
>
> **Bob** – My first category is Workshop Delivery. That is the most important part of my job.
>
> **Leader** – What do you think would be a realistic goal for that one?
>
> **Bob** – To deliver 100 days during the year. That's just over 8 days per month on average.
>
> **Leader** – And how will you do that? What are the behavioral objectives?
>
> **Bob** – Well the account executives are responsible for selling them, but in the event I am falling behind, I have another objective under the Sales Support PRC that will take care of that.
>
> **Leader** – Are there any behaviors you want feedback on?
>
> **Bob** – Yes, I have been noticing on the evaluations that participants think I'm not sensitive enough to their needs. I get rushed and forget to show empathy.
>
> **Leader** – Anything else?
>
> **Bob** – No, I think that's it for that one.
>
> **Leader** – Okay, let me recap….

Understand the available information:

> **Leader** – You want to deliver one hundred days of training for the year and get feedback on your use of empathy in the classroom. Is that right?
>
> **Bob** – Right.

Investigate alternatives:

> **Leader** – Why don't we do a little brainstorming…you said one hundred days of training. Does it matter what the mix is?
>
> **Bob** – I don't think so.
>
> **Leader** – One of the goals of the region is to increase our customizing revenue. Is that something that you would like to be involved in?
>
> **Bob** – Well, yes, that would give me an opportunity to learn how those projects are done and then provide customizing support to the region in future projects.
>
> **Leader** – So, how much of that one hundred days do you think should be devoted to customized workshops?
>
> **Bob** – Maybe ten percent or maybe twenty percent depending upon how big the project is.
>
> **Leader** – Okay, what about direct delivery vs. trainer workshops.
>
> **Bob** – Well, I prefer the trainer workshops and would want to spend sixty to eighty percent of my energy on those. I don't know…we could say sixty days on trainer, twenty days on direct delivery and twenty days on customized.
>
> **Leader** – Okay, good. I think that is reasonable. And if the mix is different because the customizing work just wasn't there, then we'll shoot for increasing the trainer workshops.
>
> **Bob** – Sounds reasonable.
>
> **Leader** – Earlier you said you get rushed and forget to show empathy. What could you do to not get rushed or to model the empathetic response?
>
> **(This continues until they have completed the brainstorming for each objective)**

Decide on the best course of action, Develop a plan, and Do it:

> **Leader** – Okay, Bob, based upon what we've discussed, why don't you summarize our agreements.

Bob – My goal for the Workshop Delivery Category is to deliver 60 days of trainer workshops, 20 days of direct delivery, and 20 days of customized workshops this year. Further, we agreed that you would provide me feedback on my use of empathy.

Leader – Good. Now, how will you track this goal?

Bob – On an excel spreadsheet.

Leader – How frequently should we meet to review progress?

Bob – I'd say once per quarter should be sufficient.

Leader – That sounds perfect. How can I help?

Bob – Just let me know if you see anything in the evaluations or personally observe me not being sensitive enough.

Leader - Okay, I will.

Evaluate progress and results, Express gratitude:

Leader – I think we have agreement on your first Performance Result Category. Let's talk about Sales Support.

(The loop continues until all PRCs and Objectives have been agreed upon. Then the leader should conclude the meeting as follows)

I think we have agreement on the plan. Thank you for your help on this, Bob. I'm confident that if you follow the plan we outlined today, you will be able to complete these expectations successfully. Why don't we meet on the 3rd of next month to review progress on your orientation conference schedule?

23

Coaching and Reinforcing Performance

INTRODUCTION

During the eleven months and twenty-nine days between the Gaining Commitment meeting and the final Performance Review, there will be many opportunities to discuss performance.

This chapter covers the following behavioral competencies:

Evaluating Results – Reviewing data on work outputs and measuring them against predetermined standards or goals. The key actions should include:

- Examining work outputs
- Holding progress review meetings
- Measuring actual performance against a standard
- Judging the quality, quantity, timeliness, and cost

Taking Corrective Action – Making adjustments to personnel or processes to ensure work is completed successfully.

- Gathering information to understand the problem
- Seeking alternative positive courses of action
- Developing action plans to ensure success

Rewarding and Disciplining – Providing incentive or punishment based upon actual performance:

- Determining the best course of action for the situation
- Administering the reward or discipline
- Scheduling a follow-up meeting

People want to accomplish or exceed the SMART Objectives they committed to during the Gaining Commitment meeting. In order to accomplish the goal, they need to understand where they are with respect to where they are going, and an acceptable way to get there.

The Progress Review meeting was scheduled during the Gaining Commitment meeting. Once you have determined whether the person is on target or not, you will conduct either a Coaching meeting or a Reinforcing meeting.

The Coaching meeting is designed to help the person through instructing or directing toward the desired result. Another opportunity for coaching occurs when the behavioral objectives are not being met.

The reinforcing meeting is the best way to encourage a person to continue a desired behavior. This meeting would occur when performance clearly exceeded expectations or is headed in that direction. After a coaching meeting; look for improvement. When you see it, reinforce it!

In the *Achieving on Purpose* cycle you are now at the point of Coaching and Reinforcing performance regularly.

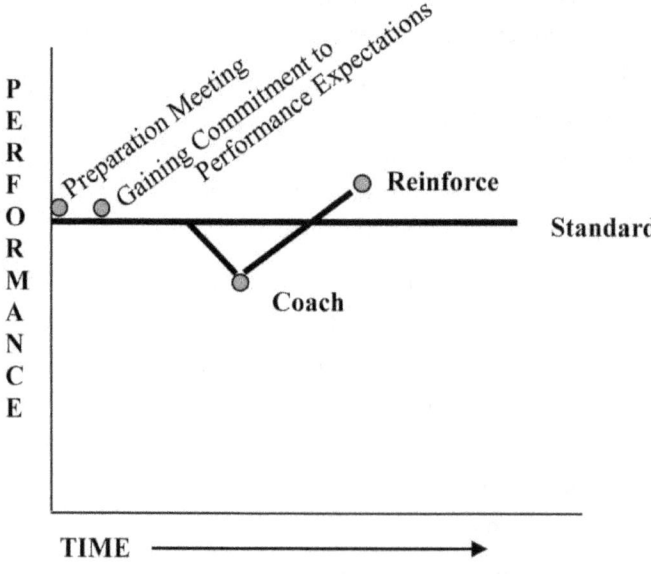

Applying GUIDE to Coaching

Prior to the meeting, ask the employee to provide any tracking documents. You'll be able to prepare for the meeting accordingly. What follows is a description of each component of the GUIDE model in the context of a coaching discussion.

Gather Information

In the context of a milestone meeting, you are seeking information about the actual performance against the plan. If there is a GAP between the actual performance and the SMART goal that was set, the problem should be framed in those terms.

In the simplest sense, gathering the following types of information helps you to take more effective action. Ask the employee to:

> ➢ Describe the actual performance
> ➢ Compare it to the SMART Objective
> ➢ Describe the cause of the gap

When you feel you have all the facts, then move on to the next step.

Understand the Available Information

As usual, this step is merely a summary of what you understand the cause of any gap might be.

At the conclusion of this step everyone involved should have a clear understanding of the current performance, the desired performance, and therefore, the GAP.

Investigate Alternatives

The most important thing to remember in this step is to seek the ideas of the employee first. Offer your ideas only after you have given the employee ample time to think. This means asking for ideas as many as seven times before you make a suggestion.

Decide on the Best Course of Action, Develop a Plan, and Do It

At this stage, I usually ask the employee to summarize the plan. That way, the person who is responsible for taking the action is making a commitment to that action. I will allow the employee to use the recommended action; unless I believe the course of action is dangerous to the employee's safety, will damage product or company property, or will undoubtedly fail.

Evaluate Progress and Results, Express Gratitude

At the conclusion of this meeting, you'll want to set a date for your next meeting that allows enough time to execute the plan. The exact amount of time depends upon the situation and how frequently the employee has an opportunity to act. If this is a daily task, I would allow a week. If this is a weekly task, perhaps a month is more reasonable. If this is a monthly task, meet next quarter. Express gratitude and confidence in the employee's ability to succeed. You might say something like:

> "When do you think we should meet to review progress?" Then add, "I'm confident that you'll be able to complete the plan, which will get you back on target. Thanks for the commitment."

Positive Model: Coaching Performance

Like the coach of a sports team, you will want to focus on what the employee can do to correct the discrepancy. If you focus on actions the employee can change, the results will likely follow. Here is a sample of what might happen during this type of discussion for a Training Manager.

Gather information:

> **Leader** – Bob, the purpose of this meeting is to review progress toward your objective of one orientation conference per quarter. Now in the first quarter you had one scheduled but it didn't happen. I've been very pleased with how you've maintained the standards on the other two Sales Support goals. What do you think might have caused this?
>
> **Bob** – Well, I'm somewhat dependent upon the Account Executives to book enough people to make the session a go.
>
> **Leader** – So, it was cancelled due to low registration?
>
> **Bob** – Right, we decided, if there were fewer than 10 people signed up, that we would cancel. There were only six.
>
> **Leader** – How many did you invite?
>
> **Bob** – I personally invited 14, but I'm pretty sure the account executives invited a lot more.
>
> **Leader** – I will check with the Account Executives, for now let's focus on the ones you invited. How did you go about it?
>
> **Bob** – I called them and let them know there was going to be a conference exclusively for clients, yada, yada, yada.
>
> **Leader** – What was the response to that?
>
> **Bob** – All but two said they would come.
>
> **Leader** – Then what did you do?
>
> **Bob** – Nothing.
>
> **Leader** – Are there any other potential causes?
>
> **Bob** – No, I think that's it.
>
> **Leader** – Okay, let me recap….

Understand the available information:

> **Leader** – You contacted 14 of your clients by phone and 12 accepted. Is that right?

Bob – Right.

Leader – How many from your list actually registered?

Bob – Three.

Leader – So three out of twelve registered.

Bob – Right.

Investigate alternatives:

Leader – Why don't we do a little brainstorming…given what we've just talked about, what ideas do you have for increasing attendance?

Bob – I guess I could call more people.

Leader – Okay, more people invited might increase the odds. Anything else?

Bob – Well, I could send a confirmation letter. That might encourage them to keep the appointment.

Leader – That's a great idea. It should impress upon them that they have made a commitment. Anything else?

Bob – I can't think of anything else.

Leader – Would it be useful to call again the day before the event?

Bob – Well, I don't want to pester them.

Leader – I can understand why you might feel like you were nagging them. Is there a way you could approach them so it wouldn't sound like pestering to them?

Bob – I guess I could say I was trying to get a final head count for catering purposes.

Leader – That sounds like it would work to me. Are there any negative consequences of doing it that way?

Bob – No I guess not.

(This continues until they have completed the brainstorming)

Decide on the best course of action, Develop a plan, and Do it:

Leader – Okay, Bob, based upon what we've discussed, why don't you summarize for me what you plan to do for your next orientation conference?

Bob – First, I will send out invitations to the entire client database, without censoring anyone out. Then, I will have the Account Executives contact them by phone to remind them to look for something in the mail. Then the day before, I will contact everyone who signed up to confirm head count.

Leader – That sounds great. I expect you will get a much better response with that strategy. Is there anything else you need from me?

Bob – I don't think so. This was a big help.

Evaluate progress and results, Express gratitude:

Leader – All right, I think we have agreement on a plan. Thank you for your help on this, Bob. I'm confident that if you follow the plan we outlined today, you will be able to reach your goal successfully. When should we meet again on this, before the orientation or after?

Bob – Let's plan to meet the day after the conference. With the contingency that if we don't have enough registrations by, say two weeks before, we could talk about what to do. Okay?

Leader – Okay, the conference is on the 21st of January. So, we will meet on the 22nd, unless there is a problem with registration.

Applying GUIDE to Reinforcing

The assumption going into this meeting is that the employee has corrected the problem and is now back on target to reach goals set for the year. What follows is a description of each component of the GUIDE model in the context of a reinforcing discussion.

Gather Information

In the context of a reinforcing meeting, you are seeking information about the actual performance and how the person was able to make the changes necessary to succeed.

Basically, this is all praise related. Ask questions that allow the employee to bask in his moment of glory:

> "How did you do it?"
> "What made the biggest difference?"

Sometimes the employee will be humble, not wanting to brag. If that happens just move on.

Understand the Available Information

This step is your summary of what happened. The most important thing to do here is be complementary. Add anything the employee may not know, such as, complements from other employees or customers.

Investigate Alternatives

Skip this step, even if the employee wants to discuss how to make things better. Suggest scheduling another meeting to discuss improvements. This meeting should be nothing but positive reinforcement.

Decide on the Best Course of Action, Develop a Plan, and Do It

Skip this step as well.

Evaluate Progress and Results, Express Gratitude

Express gratitude. That's all. You might say something like:

> "If you handle this the same way next time, you'll be just as successful."

Positive Model: Reinforcing Performance

Specific and sincere reinforcement means honest feedback that encourages a person to continue the desired behavior. Here is a sample of what might happen during this type of discussion with a Training Manager.

Gather information:

> **Leader** – Bob, looks like your orientation conference went extremely well. How many were in attendance?
>
> **Bob** – We had 47.
>
> **Leader** – That's quite an increase from last time.
>
> **Bob** – I'll say…we had to cancel the last one because there were only six registrants.
>
> **Leader** – What did you do differently?
>
> **Bob** – I followed our plan. When I sent out the invitations to people, even if they were outside the state, I really thought that it would be a waste of time. But we got half-a-dozen or so who flew in to attend. And, the follow-up calls helped. Several people said they would have forgotten all about it if I hadn't called to remind them.

Understand the available information:

> **Leader** – Well it sounds like your strategy really paid off. I also heard from Harry. He said because of the way you handled the orientation, he has three more commitments to purchase the new Serving on Purpose program.
>
> **Bob** – That's great.

Investigate alternatives:

Decide on the best course of action, Develop a plan, and Do it:

Evaluate progress and results, Express gratitude:

> **Leader** – I'm impressed with the way you handled the entire conference, congratulations. Also, if you handle it this same way next time, it will really help you make your annual target.

24

Motivating Through Performance Review

INTRODUCTION

The formal performance appraisal has two purposes. First, it's important to document the progress the employee made toward each PRC. This completes the cycle that was started with the Gaining Commitment event at the beginning of the year. Second, it provides the opportunity to begin the cycle again by building on the past performance. You'll want to set similar objectives for the coming year.

This chapter covers the following behavioral competencies:

Evaluating Results – Reviewing data on work outputs and measuring them against predetermined standards or goals. The key actions should include:

- ➤ Examining work outputs
- ➤ Holding progress review meetings
- ➤ Measuring actual performance against a standard
- ➤ Judging the quality, quantity, timeliness, and cost

Developing Performance Standards – Using appropriate interpersonal styles to guide the development of work expectations:

- ➤ Clarifying expected performance, goals, and objectives
- ➤ Seeking involvement from the employee
- ➤ Gaining genuine agreement and enthusiasm for targets
- ➤ Documenting the plan for tracking purposes

In reviewing performance, you'll be calculating the final totals for actual performance and comparing them to the targets. You'll want to discuss why performance expectations were met in order to continue reaching or exceeding them. You will also want to explore why performance elements were not met, so you can modify the plan in some way.

In the *Achieving on Purpose* cycle you are now at the point of Motivating through Performance Review.

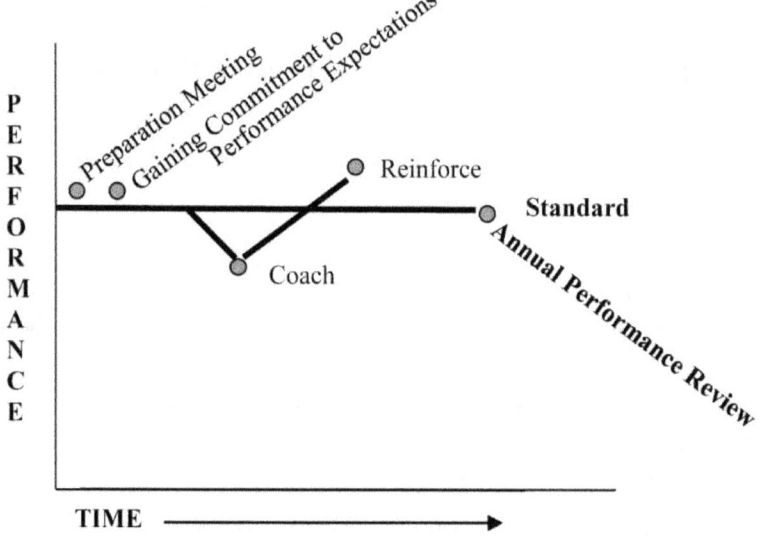

Applying GUIDE to Motivating Through Performance Review

Using GUIDE while reviewing performance helps keep you focused on the task part of your interaction. It ensures that you clarify the objective of the interaction and maintain focus as you proceed to the desired outcome. What follows is a description of each component of the GUIDE model in the context of a performance review discussion.

*G*ather Information

The first step in the performance review is to gather information about actual performance versus the expected performance. Essentially, the leader asks what the result was for each objective and compares that to the expectation.

There are only three outcomes:

1. The expectation was exceeded
2. The expectation was met
3. The expectation was not met

Once the result is known, the leader needs to uncover the reason for success or failure, the why, the cause. There are four things to consider:

Coincidental Factors – Anything outside the employee's control that helped or hindered in accomplishing the desired result.

The SMART Objective – Sometimes, the performance expected isn't realistic, clear, or controllable. Sometimes you may want to raise the bar; to increase the expectation and challenge the employee to greater performance.

Actions or Skills Used – Performance targets could have been met due to the actions of the employee, there may have been some skills the employee has that weren't used, or there may be some skills the employee needs to be trained to use.

Your Own Behavior – The manager may have done something that helped or hindered performance.

When you feel you have all the facts on the first objective; then move on to the next step. You will want to go through the GUIDE process for each objective or each PRC depending upon how the objectives are linked to the PRC. That means at least one loop for each PRC, maybe more.

*U*nderstand the Available Information

Summarize your understanding of the reason why the employee succeeded or failed.

---

*I*nvestigate Alternatives

There are only three choices with every SMART or Behavioral Objective based upon the situation:

1. Keep it the same for next year
2. Change it for next year
3. Eliminate it from the list

*D*ecide on the Best Course of Action, *D*evelop a Plan, and *D*o It

Ask the employee to summarize what the goals will be for the coming year, how it will be tracked and when to review progress.

*E*valuate Progress and Results, *E*xpress Gratitude

At the conclusion of this meeting, you will want to set a date for your next meeting and express gratitude. The next meeting will be a milestone check which gives you the opportunity to coach or reinforce on a specific goal or objective.

> "I think we have agreement on a plan. Thank you for your diligence. Why don't we meet in two weeks, say on the 21st to discuss your progress with the customer service goal?

Expressing gratitude acknowledges contributions and ceremoniously brings the GUIDE journey to an end.

Positive Model: Motivating Through Performance Review

Motivating someone through the performance review process can be very rewarding. Here is a sample of what might happen during this type of discussion with a Training Manager.

Gather Information:

> **Leader** – Bob, the purpose of this meeting is to review your performance over the year so that we can learn from it to plan for next year. The payoff for you will be to help improve your performance, increase your confidence in controlling your job, and decrease effort on unnecessary activities. Are you ready to begin?

> **Bob** – I'm ready.

> **Leader** – Great! I thought we'd take one PRC at a time, discuss the SMART Objectives and the Behavioral Objectives, come to an agreement and then come back to the next PRC. Does that sound Okay? How do you feel about the process?

> **Bob** – Fine, sounds good.

> **Leader** – Let's take your first PRC. You goal-set to deliver one hundred days. How did you actually do?

> **Bob** – I met the goal.

> **Leader** – Excellent, I can see that you are pleased! Now, it's important for us to determine why you met the goal; so, we can repeat it…were there any coincidental factors that I should be aware of?

> **Bob** – Well, as you know a lot depends on the Account Executives to sell the training. They did their job, which allowed me to do mine.

> **Leader** – So, what did you actually do?

> **Bob** – I delivered one hundred and seven days. Eighty were trainer workshops, fifteen were direct delivery, and twelve were part of a customizing workshop for Wyndham International Resorts.

> **Leader** – I know you enjoyed getting to go to Puerto Rico. How did I help or hinder?

> **Bob** – The best thing you did for me was coach me on looking for opportunities to show empathy. My evaluations have been consistently positive ever since.

> **Leader** – I'm happy you were able to improve that. Great job! Anything else?

Bob – No, I think that's it for that one.

Leader – Okay, let me recap.

Understand the available information:

> **Leader** – You delivered one hundred and seven days of training for the year and the mix was eighty, fifteen, and twelve days, respectively. This is slightly over the target for trainer workshops and slightly under for the other two, but clearly within the ranges we discussed. Also, your evaluations have gone up in the area of sensitivity. Is that right?
>
> **Bob** – Right.

Investigate alternatives:

> **Leader** – So what do you think the goal should be for the coming year?
>
> **Bob** – I'd like to keep it the same.
>
> **Leader** – Will that be challenging enough for you?
>
> **Bob** – Well, yes, I think so.
>
> **Leader** – So, the goal was sixty, twenty, and twenty with some leeway to account for coincidental factors out of your immediate control.
>
> **Bob** – I think that sounds realistic.
>
> **Leader** – All right, I agree. Now, what about the behavioral objectives? Is there anything you want to work on in that regard?
>
> **Bob** – I don't think so.
>
> **Leader** – I'd like to see you get a full twenty days of direct delivery, particularly in the courses where your experience is less. What do you think you could do to increase the opportunities?
>
> **Bob** – Well, I guess I could do a little more cross selling at the end of the trainer workshops. You know, to let them know we are available for that kind of thing.
>
> **Leader** – That sounds like a good idea. How can I help you with that?
>
> **Bob** – You could watch me rehearse and give me feedback.
>
> **Leader** – I would be available anytime.
>
> **(This continues until they have completed the brainstorming for each objective)**

Decide on the best course of action, Develop a plan, and Do it:

> **Leader** – Okay, Bob, based upon what we've discussed, summarize for me our agreements.

> **Bob** – My goal for the Workshop Delivery Category is to deliver sixty days of trainer workshops, twenty days of direct delivery, and twenty days of customized workshops this year. Further, we agreed that you would provide me feedback on my cross-selling presentation.

> **Leader** – How will you track this goal?

> **Bob** – My excel spread-sheet.

> **Leader** – How frequently should we meet to review progress?

> **Bob** – I'd say once per quarter should be sufficient.

> **Leader** – That sounds perfect. How can I help?

> **Bob** – Just let me know if you see anything in the evaluations or personally observe something that could be improved.

> **Leader** - Okay, I will.

Evaluate progress and results, Express gratitude:

> **Leader** – I think we have agreement on your first Performance Result Category. Let's talk about Sales Support.

> **(The loop continues until all PRCs and Objectives have been agreed upon. Then the leader should conclude the meeting as follows)**

> I think we have agreement on the plan. Thank you for your help on this, Bob. I'm confident that if you follow the plan we outlined today, you will be able to complete these expectations successfully. Why don't we meet next week to review your cross-selling plans, say on Wednesday?

Appendices

APPENDIX A

Commit Coaching Tips

Give authority where appropriate.   **Don't remove responsibility.**

Asking for Involvement

"What ideas do you have about…?"

"What responsibility do you see yourself taking on?"

"What parts of this project are you interested in spearheading?"

"Can I count on your help?"

"I need your help in solving this problem."

Offering Your Involvement

"How can I help you complete this project?"

"I'm committed to doing what it takes."

"What resources do you need from me?"

"You know you can count on my support."

Things You Can Do to Show Commitment

Share important information (memos, articles, etc.).

Provide names and numbers of people who can help.

Do—*today*— what you say you will do in the future (don't procrastinate).
Don't put off until tomorrow what you can do today.

*A*ffirm Coaching Tips

Affirm others' value.   Maintain others' self-esteem.   Use what and why statements.

>"I know you can do [this] because I've seen you do [something similar] before."
>
>   what   why

>"I'm glad you're on my team. You have a lot to offer.
>
>   what   why

>"It's good to have you working on [this]. You give [this] a fresh approach."
>
>   what   why

>"You are so good with numbers. I need someone like you on [this]."
>
>   what   why

>"I was hoping I'd see you today. Could you look at something I've been working on?"
>
>   what   why

>"You have such a unique perspective. We're glad you agreed to volunteer."
>
>   what   why

Things You Can Do To Affirm Others:

>Hug
>
>Find opportunities to "toot other's horn"
>
>Take someone "for a SPIN"

*R*ecognize Coaching Tips

Recognize accomplishments   **Bolster self-esteem**

      WHAT   WHY

"Congratulations on your new job! It's appropriate, for improving profits by twenty percent."

"You got the program done. This helps exceed our customers' expectations."

"Outstanding performance on the McKnight project! The whole thing flowed seamlessly."

"Great presentation on the need for empathy. It touched my heart."

"The New Insurance slide show was very informative. Employees are overjoyed."

"Your CI project saved six percent of rework. Thanks! Quality is our number one goal."

Things you can do to recognize others:

Tell others

Write thank you notes

Take someone "for a SPIN"

*E*mpathize Coaching Tips

Recognize Situation and Emotions   **Listen more, speak less.**

> **"Completing that project** has got to be *a relief.*"
> **Situation**   *Emotion*

> "I know how *frustrating* it is **to be let down** like that."
> *Emotion*   **Situation**

> "Congratulations on your **new job**. That's got to *feel good.*"
> **Situation**   *Emotion*

> "It can be *embarrassing* to **miss a meeting**."
> *Emotion*   **Situation**

> "You've been **planning this trip** for months and it's here. How *exciting*
> for you!"
> **Situation**   *Emotion*

> "Are you *disheartened* about **the response to your survey**?"
> *Emotion*   **Situation**

Things you can do to show empathy:

> Write a personal note
>
> Offer help or support in solving the problem

APPENDIX B

---------------------- ϫ ----------------------

Planning GUIDE

*G*ather information
Who, what, where, how, when, why regarding history of plans in this area

*C*ommit
*A*ffirm
*R*ecognize
*E*mpathize

*U*nderstand the available information
Check for understanding, who would know?

*I*nvestigate alternatives
List all possible activities based upon what MUST happen. Who could/should do it? When is it possible?

*D*ecide on the best course of action, Develop a plan, and Do it
Finalize action steps in chronological order. Assign responsibilities. Who will do What by When? Establish completion dates for each step, working backwards, and allocate resources.

Ask what could go wrong & develop contingencies.

*E*valuate progress and results, Express gratitude
Track progress, evaluate, make corrections, and continuously improve. Thank those involved.

Organizing GUIDE

Gather information

Who, what, when, where, how, why regarding history of organizational structures, job qualifications and position descriptions in your area/department/team.

> **Commit**
> **Affirm**
> **Recognize**
> **Empathize**

Understand the available information

Check for understanding. Who would know?

Investigate alternatives

List all possible options based upon your organizing task.

Decide on the best course of action, Develop a plan, and Do it

Develop Organization Charts, Job Descriptions, Interview Guides, etc. Decide what actions come first, second, etc.

Evaluate progress and results, Express gratitude

Track progress, evaluate, make corrections, and continuously improve. Thank those involved.

ProblemSolving GUIDE

*G*ather information
What's the problem? Where does it exist? When did you first notice it?
What is the scope?

Commit
*A*ffirm
*R*ecognize
*E*mpathize

*U*nderstand the available information
Check for understanding (yours and theirs). What's unique? What's been altered? Is your hypothesis logical?

*I*nvestigate alternatives
State the purpose. Determine decision criteria. Determine relative importance of desirables. List the alternatives. Determine which alternative best meets the need.

*D*ecide on the best course of action, Develop a plan, and Do it
Choose the best alternative as compared to the decision criteria. Don't hesitate.

*E*valuate progress and results, Express gratitude
Evaluate what could go wrong and consider contingencies.

Influencing GUIDE

Gather information
Seek audience input 1st Offer your input 2nd Tell story, shocking example, dramatic statistic

> *Commit*
> *Affirm*
> *Recognize*
> *Empathize*

Understand the available information
Summarize why the problem exist, is significant   Check for agreement

Investigate alternatives
Seek ideas to solve the issue or provide specific, viable solutions

Decide on the best course of action, Develop a plan, and Do it
Tell the audience what will happen if the solution is implemented versus not; then, call for action

Evaluate progress and results, Express gratitude
Thank audience for meeting.   Express confidence in carrying out the solution

Discussion GUIDE

Gather information
Seek staff input 1st Offer your input 2nd Facts, data, stats, dates, projects
worked on/completed.... Focus on job not the person

> **C**ommit
> **A**ffirm
> **R**ecognize
> **E**mpathize

Understand the available information
You believe...   You feel...   Agree or agree to disagree?   Summarize
Check for understanding (yours & theirs)

Investigate alternatives
"What ideas do you have about...?"   Use or build on staff ideas when possible   Offer own ideas last

Decide on the best course of action, Develop a plan, and Do it
Who, what, when, where, why, how

Set follow-up dates/times

Evaluate progress and results, Express gratitude
"Thanks for meeting with me today. I appreciate your input. You're a valuable contributor...   I found
this helpful. Did this meet your expectations? "

Bibliography

BIBLIOGRAPHY

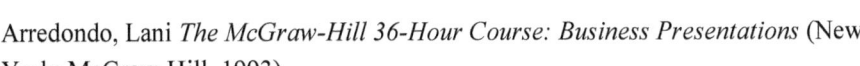

Arredondo, Lani *The McGraw-Hill 36-Hour Course: Business Presentations* (New York: McGraw-Hill, 1993).

Bates, Jefferson D. *Writing with Precision* (Washington, D.C.: Acropolis Books, 1978).

Bennett, Joel B. and Steinbrecher, Susan *Heart-Centered Leadership An Invitation to Lead from the Inside Out* (Memphis: Black Pants Publishing, 2003). www.instituteofhcl.com

Blanchard, Ken et.al. *Empowerment Takes More Than a Minute* (San Francisco: Berrett-Koehler Publishers, 1996).

Blanchard, Ken et.al. *The 3 Keys to Empowerment* (San Francisco: Berrett-Koehler Publishers, 1999).

Brassard, Michael and Ritter, Diane *The Memory Jogger II* (Methuen, MA: GOAL/QPC, 1994).

Bright, Stephen *The Prelude* (Elsternwick, Australia: Catalyst Communication Consultants, 1989).

Byham, William C. with Debra Pickett *Landing the Job You Want* (Pittsburgh: DDI Press, 1997).

Byham, William C. with Steven M. Krauzer *The Selection Solution* (Pittsburgh: DDI Press, 1996).

Byham, William C. with Jeff Cox *Zapp! The Lightning of Empowerment* (Pittsburgh: DDI Press, 1989).

Crosby, Phillip B. *Quality is Free* (New York: New American Library, 1979).

Davis, Brian L. et. al. *Successful Manager's Handbook* (Minneapolis: Personnel Decisions, Inc., 1989).

Doyle, Michael and Straus, David *How to Make Meetings Work* (New York: Jove Books, 1976).

Drucker, Peter F. *Innovation and Entrepreneurship* (New York: HarperBusiness, 1985).

Drucker, Peter F. *Managing for Results* (New York: HaperBusiness, 1986).

Fisher, R., & Ury, W. *Getting to Yes: Negotiating Agreement Without Giving In.* (New York: Penguin Books, 1981).

Goleman, Daniel *Emotional Intelligence: Why It Can Matter More Than IQ* (New York: Bantam Books, 1995).

Hammer, M. and Champy, J. *Reengineering the Corporation* (New York: Harper Collins, 1993).

Harvey, Jerry B. *The Abilene Paradox* (New York: Lexington Books, 1988).

Heller, Robert and Hindle, Tim *Essential Manager's Manual* (New York: DK Publishing, Inc., 1998).

Hersey, Paul and Blanchard, Kenneth H. *Management of Organizational Behavior: Utilizing Human Resources* (Englewood Cliffs, New Jersey: Prentice-Hall, Inc., 1982).

Hodges, John C. and Whitten, Mary E. *Harbrace College Handbook 6th Edition* (New York: Harcourt, Brace & World, Inc., 1967).

Huszczo, Gregory E. *Tools for Team Leadership* (Palo Alto: Davies-Black Publishing, 2004).

Imai, Masaaki *Kaizen* (New York: McGraw-Hill, 1986).

Janis, Irving L. *Groupthink* (Boston: Houghton Mifflin Company 1982).

Kepner, Charles H. and Tregoe, Benjamin B. *The Rational Manager: A Systematic Approach to Problem Solving and Decision Making* (Princeton: Kepner-Tregoe, Inc., 1965).

Kotter, John P. *Leading Change* (Boston: Harvard Business School Press, 1996).

Kotter, John P. *The Heart of Change* (Boston: Harvard Business School Press, 2002).

Kouzes, James M. and Posner, Barry Z. *The Leadership Challenge: How to Get Extraordinary Things Done in Organizations* (San Francisco: Jossey-Bass Publishers, 1987).

Krayer, Karl J. and Lee, William W. *Organizing Change* (San Francisco: Jossey-Bass, 2003).

Land, George and Jarman, Beth *Breakpoint and Beyond* (New York: Harper Business, 1992).

Lefton, Robert E., et.al. *Effective Motivation Through Performance Appraisal* (St. Louis: Psychological Associates, 1977).

Lencioni, Patrick *The FIVE Dysfunctions of a TEAM* (San Francisco: Jossey-Bass, 2002).

Mackenzie, R. Alec *The Time Trap* (New York: McGraw-Hill, 1972).

Mager, Robert F. and Pipe, Peter *Analyzing Performance Problems or 'You Really Oughta Wanna'* (Belmont: Fearon-Pitman Publishers, Inc., 1970).

Miller, William C. *The Creative Edge* (New York: Addison-Wesley, 1987).

Mink, Oscar G. *An Introduction to Action Research* (Austin: Somerset Consulting Group, 1992).

Mink, Oscar G. et al *Change at Work* (San Francisco: Jossey-Bass, 1993).

Newman, Edwin, *Strictly Speaking* (New York: Warner Books, 1980).

Oja, Sharon Nodie and Smulyan, Lisa *Collaborative Action Research: A Developmental Approach* (New York: Falmer Press, 1989).

Pande, Peter S. et al *The Six Sigma Way* (New York: McGraw-Hill, 2000).

Patterson, Kerry, et. al. *Crucial Conversations* (New York: McGraw-Hill, 2002).

Senge, Peter M. *The Fifth Discipline* (New York: Doubleday Currency, 1990).

Tichy, Noel M. and Bennis, Warren G. *JUDGMENT* (New York: Penguin Group, 2007).

Zenger, John H. and Stinnett, Kathleen *The Extraordinary Coach: How the Best Leaders Help Others Grow* (New York: McGraw-Hill, 2010).